TABLE OF CONTENTS

PART ONE

UNDERSTANDING THE PROBLEM

An Introduction to Learning Disabilities and the Environmental Influences that Impact the Childs Ability to Learn

CHALLENGES IN THE CLASSROOM

Signs and Symptoms of Learning Disabilities

with Accommodations and Modifications

for Home and School

Chapter

INTRODUCTION

Learning disabilities have many names and faces as well as many causes and ways in which they manifest in the learning styles of children. To explore them all would take volumes of information, much of which is not relevant to the needs of parents, the intended audience for this effort. This work, while written by an academician, is an uncomplicated resource for information that will serve as a quick study for parents who have been introduced to the concept of special education for the first time.

While students and professionals may find this information controversial, they too may gain some insight into environmental influences upon learning, which may serve them well during the assessment process.

Part I is an introduction to the environmental influences since World War II that are believed to be contributing to the incidence of learning disabilities that is increasing at a rate of 10 to 20% every 10 years.

Some of the social practices having the most negative influence upon child development are identified. Incidence in the population and impact upon learning are reported as each chapter seeks to answer the likely questions: Why Is This Happening? What Does This Mean for My Child? Activities, interventions, accommodations and modifications to facilitate learning, both at home and at school, are offered at the end of each chapter in a section entitled What to Do.

Part II includes a definition and history of special education and its intended role and function in the effort to educate all children. The reader is introduced to the process of determining eligibility for special education and Federal and state legislation is explored in terms of the parent's rights in the process. The responsibility of the school district and some explanation of the discrepancy between what the law says and what the schools are doing are examined. Further, it explains why the schools are not always able to abide by the spirit and letter of the law.

Part III is an exploration of processing disorders, as required for a designation of learning disability. Behaviors exhibited in the classroom and a rationale for the behavior, along with modifications and accommodations for the general education classroom, are offered. These interventions are applied to the elementary, middle school and high school environments as an aid in developing the Individualized Education Plan (IEP).

Finally, some liberty has been taken to be candid about child-rearing practices in modern America, the attitudes of teachers and schools toward children needing special education and to share with parents the many things about children, education and the law about which it is not in the school's best interest for them to know.

Overall, this work is a road map of how-to activities, which will be of assistance from the beginning to the end of the special education process. The information contained herein is intended to assist parents in making a decision about whether to place their child in special education, as well as show them some ways to assist the learning process at home and in the general education classroom as the least restrictive environment. Also, it may be of some help to parents who already have made the decision and have placed—or refused to place—their child in special education.

The objective of this work is to assist parents and professionals in assuring that each child receives a "free, appropriate, public education" by building an educational program around identified learning strengths and weaknesses while seeking an answer to the question: "is special education appropriate, even if the child is eligible?"

ENDORSEMENT

Learning problems are almost invisible outside the classroom. Yet, they are profound and make life incredibly difficult for the children who live with them. Families and teachers of these children are equally challenged.

This book is a rare gem of literature which provides support to families and teachers that will have an immediate, direct impact upon the lives of children.

As a child I experienced the kind of learning problems addressed in this manual, but was lucky to have the support I needed at home and school. With this support I was able to successfully complete public school and earn a graduate degree at the University of California. Most children with learning difficulties are not so lucky.

Successful approaches only require that parents and teachers learn a few principles and use them to teach and support children who may seem uncooperative even when they are trying to learn. This book describes those principles and approaches and offers valuable guidelines to improve the lives and academic success of children with learning disabilities.

Changing the outcomes from failure to success does not require great economic sacrifice and expensive therapies. Simple changes in childrearing practices, diet and nutrition, exercise and parents actively involved in their child's education are all that is required.

This practical book outlines what causes learning disabilities and then offers ways to prevent or remediate the problem in 98% of the children with learning problems.

For children with more complicated psycho-neurological disabilities, suggested modifications and accommodations are equally effective and should be instituted early and maintained throughout the child's education.

I was lucky. Most children are not. This information, if utilized, is certain to improve the outcomes for children of the twenty-first century.

Anita L. King, LCSW

Licensed Clinical Social Worker

CHAPTER I

LEARNING DISABILITIES

Being told that your child is not learning well and may have a learning disability can be a very disturbing event. The first questions that come to mind are: What is a learning disability? What causes a learning disability? What does this mean for my child? Now what do I do?

What is a Learning Disability?

In the United States and Canada the term learning disability (LD) refers to a group of disorders that affect a broad range of academic and functional skills. Currently almost 1.9 million school-aged children in the US are classified as having specific learning disabilities and receive some kind of special education support, and these numbers do not include children in private and religious schools or home-schooled children.

The common characteristic about these children is that they have difficulty learning. Otherwise, they are uniquely individual in their learning styles and abilities. These unique differences do not prevent learning they simply require special teaching methods.

Usually these special methods have to be adapted to the strengths and weaknesses and unique learning style of each individual child. Because they are adapted to special needs, programs designed to meet these special needs are called special education.

Learning problems that are primarily the result of poor vision or hearing, motor disabilities, mental retardation, autism, emotional disturbance, or environmental, cultural or economic disadvantage may be eligible for special services but are not considered to be a learning disability. For a child to be identified as having a learning disability he must meet very specific criteria outlined by law.

Legal Definition of a Learning Disability

In order to be identified as having a learning disability, a child must demonstrate average or above average intelligence, and the child's level of achievement must be significantly below what his average intelligence would suggest that he should be able to achieve.

The law states that a significant discrepancy must exist between intellectual ability and level of achievement. Achievement and intellect must be measured by standardized tests in the following areas:

- Oral Expression
- Written Expression
- Basic Reading skills
- Reading Comprehension
- Mathematical calculation
- Mathematical reasoning

The severe discrepancy between ability and achievement must be due to a deficit in one or more of the following basic psychological processes:

- Attention
- Visual Processing
- Auditory Processing
- Sensori-motor skills
- Cognitive abilities including association, conceptualization and expression

How Learning Disabilities are Identified

Given the above guidelines, learning disabilities are identified by a combination of intelligence testing, academic achievement testing, classroom performance, social interaction and aptitude. Other areas of assessment may include perception, cognition, memory, attention, and language abilities. Test outcomes depend not only on the child's actual abilities, but on the reliability of the test and the child's ability to pay attention and understand the questions.

Each type of learning disability is diagnosed in slightly different ways. To diagnose speech and language disorders, a speech therapist tests the child's pronunciation, vocabulary, and grammar and compares them to the developmental abilities seen in most children of the same age. A psychologist tests the child's intelligence. A physician checks for any ear infections, and an audiologist may be consulted to rule out hearing problems. If the problem involves articulation, a doctor examines the child's vocal cords and throat.

In the case of academic skill disorders, academic development in reading, writing, and math is evaluated using standardized tests. In addition, vision and hearing are tested to be sure that the student can see words clearly and can hear adequately. The specialist also checks the child's school attendance to be sure that he has received sufficient instruction to be able to achieve at grade level. Once the evaluation is complete, the basic approach is to teach learning skills by building on the child's abilities and strengths while correcting and compensating for disabilities and weaknesses.

Causes of Learning Disabilities

At one time, scientists thought that all learning disabilities were caused by a single neurological problem, but research has demonstrated that the causes are more diverse and complex. New evidence seems to show that most learning disabilities do not stem from a single, specific area of the brain, but from difficulties in bringing together information from various parts of the brain. A leading theory today is that learning disabilities stem from subtle disturbances in brain structures and functions. While learning disabilities are very real limiting conditions in the central nervous system which significantly impact the ability to learn, there is overwhelming evidence that most forms of learning disability are caused by trauma. The trauma, either unidentified or neglected, interferes with the normal development of the central nervous system, or prevents its normal function.

Some possible causes may be due to heredity. Often learning disabilities run in families, so it is not uncommon to find that people with learning disabilities have parents or other relatives with similar difficulties. Learning disabilities may be caused by illness or injury during or before birth. They may also be caused by drug and alcohol use during pregnancy, low birth weight, lack of oxygen and premature or prolonged labor.

Head injuries, nutritional deprivation and exposure to toxic substances can also contribute to learning disabilities. Natural disaster, grief, loss or abandonment by a non-nurturing parent, or child abuse and neglect are all distressing experiences which may lead to learning disabilities.

There are other more serious injuries to the central nervous system which cause learning problems, but these injuries are not classified as learning disabilities. Other designations identified as eligible for special education include other health impaired, emotionally disturbed, deaf or hard of hearing, mentally handicapped, auditory processing disorder, language impaired, and physically handicapped.

Evidence suggests that even these more serious conditions can be modified with proper intervention, or they could have been prevented with proper care. Therefore, while emphasis in this writing is upon learning disabilities, many of the accommodations suggested at the end of each chapter apply equally as well to other conditions requiring special education.

What Does This Mean for My Child

While learning disabilities are not uncommon, they appear to be more common in boys than in girls.[i] There are many theories about why this is so, but none have been proven conclusively. Both boys and girls have similar experiences with learning difficulties and their consequences.

A learning disability is not just a minor problem that simply goes away as a child matures. These conditions must be identified and treated early. If they are, there is a greater chance that children having difficulty learning will reach their potential. Teachers and parents must work together to help students with learning disabilities to develop the skills that they need. A recent report from the National Institutes of Health showed that 67% of young students who were at risk for reading difficulties became average or above-average readers after receiving help in the early grades.

Early intervention prevents the development of more serious learning problems resulting from long-term neglect and/or untreated trauma. In the event that the trauma continues over a long period of time and brings about significant change in behavior, the problem may require a change in designation. For example, a neglected or abused child may have learning problems, but with continued neglect and abuse, the child's psychology and inappropriate behaviors may require a change in designation from learning disabled to emotionally disturbed.

What to Do

Mental health professionals stress that because there is no common agreement as to what causes learning disabilities; it doesn't help parents to look backward to search for possible reasons. There are too many possibilities to pin down the cause of the disability with certainty. It is far more important for the family to move forward in finding ways to get the right help. The brain is a vital, alive, dynamic organ and has been known to regenerate when the stressor has been removed or with appropriate therapeutic intervention.

Specific educational assistance is the best intervention for individuals with learning disabilities. Remedial training in areas where a disabled child is weakest is best managed by trained teachers, reading specialists, or tutors in special classes or schools.

In order to develop a comprehensive approach for each child, the law requires any school receiving Federal aid for education to develop Individual Education Plans for all children requiring a special education. Parents are encouraged to participate in the process of designing the individualized education plan. Parents are additionally encouraged to become involved in rearing children in an environment free of trauma that may have the potential of interfering with the child's developing central nervous system.

That is why you, as a parent, school psychologist, therapist or other practitioner, will want to explore the exact nature of the child's problem. Talk with teachers about what the child is doing in the classroom, observe the child's behavior, find what is contributing to the behavior and then address the problem by investigating to make sure that the problem is not caused by some environmental condition which should be addressed with proper modifications and accommodations at home and/or in the classroom.

Statistics suggest that large numbers of families with handicapped children wind up in divorce. Don't become so involved with the handicapped child that you neglect the rest of the family and particularly your marriage. More than ever, your learning-disabled child needs an intact family to love, support and get him through these trying times.

CHAPTER II

ENVIRONMENTAL INFLUENCES

The following chapters identify some conditions that contribute to processing disorders in the central nervous system. Consider these chapters a survival manual for the identification of, and intervention with some of the most prevalent sources of environmental trauma contributing to the development of disorders which interfere with learning. Examination of these environmental conditions provides a better understanding of the nature of learning disabilities and why they are increasing at a rate of 10 to 20% every 10 years.   Since it does not appear that the human race is devolving rapidly enough to attribute the increase to heredity, it seems logical to explore the environment as a contributing factor. Upon investigation many factors in the environment have been found to have a significant impact upon the development of the neural structures involved with learning. When these structures are not completely developed or are impacted by trauma, many weaknesses in the ability to learn become evident in the classroom.

An understanding of the central nervous system and other systems that interact with it to enable the functions of hearing, seeing, reading and learning will be helpful in understanding the processing disorders usually labeled as learning disabilities.

The Central Nervous System   The central nervous system is that part of the human body that includes the brain and the spinal cord. The brain and spinal cord are the most vital parts of the human body. These two structures are enclosed in bone which protects them from injury. The brain is encased in the cranium (skull) and the spinal cord is encased in the vertebrae of the spine.

Image

Brain and Spinal Cord

The bones of the cranium are in constant motion, moving only ever so slightly, and are involved in the process of normal physiological processes such as respiration, cardiac (the heart) activity and movement of the cerebrospinal fluid. Concussions to the head at any age can and will traumatize this delicate cranium bone movement as well as potentially cause a brain tissue injury. When the cranium or spine is traumatized it can have cascading effects throughout the nervous system, resulting in functional impairments that can be disabling.

Forty-two bones form the spinal column. Between each of these bones, nerves leave the spinal column and govern the majority of the large skeletal muscles of the body. In addition to the nerves that control muscles, there is an even greater concentration of nerves that funnel information gathered from the thousands 5f sensors in the skin muscles and joints and transmit it back to the brain through these same spinal nerves. The brain receives additional information through the vestibular, visual and auditory systems.

The Vestibular System

The vestibular is the first sensory system to fully develop. It is the system that controls the sense of movement and balance. This system is the sensory system considered to have the most important influence on the other sensory systems and on the ability to function in everyday life. Directly or indirectly, the vestibular system influences nearly everything we do. It is the unifying system in our brain that modifies and coordinates information received from other systems. Ninety percent of the cells on the visual cortex of the brain respond to vestibular stimulation. Smell, taste and touch are the only three modalities of human processing that are relatively unaffected by vestibular function.

The sense organs for the vestibular system are located within the inner ear and consist of three semicircular canals which arch in three different directions so that they are able to register movement of the head in all directions. Projections from the vestibular system to other parts of the brain and sensory organs serve as communication channels. Through these channels, the vestibular system influences the autonomic nervous system, governs auditory functions, visual functions, muscle tone, balance and sense of direction in space.

Image

The Vestibular Apparatus

The vestibular apparatus

The Auditory System

This system also has its receptors in the inner ear and is heavily involved with the vestibular system. The vestibular and auditory nerves join in the auditory canal and become the eighth cranial nerve of the brain. As a consequence, anything that disrupts auditory information can also affect vestibular functioning and vice-versa. This system is responsible for the process of hearing and is comprised of the outer ear, middle ear and the inner ear.

The outer ear consists of folds of cartilage surrounding a long tube called the ear canal. These cartilages reflect sound waves, which provide information that will help the brain determine the direction from which the sound comes. At the far end of the ear canal is the eardrum, which marks the beginning of the middle ear.

Sound waves vibrate through the eardrum and travel across the air-filled middle ear cavity via a series of delicate bones called the ossicles. These bones in some miraculous manner convert the lower-pressure eardrum sound vibrations into higher-pressure sound vibrations at another smaller membrane called the oval window. Higher pressure is necessary because the inner ear beyond the oval window contains fluid rather than air. If the sound is not amplified uniformly across the ossicle chain, the auditory reflex of the middle ear muscles help protect the inner ear from damage. In the middle ear, the sound information is still in wave form and is converted to nerve impulses in the inner ear.

The inner ear consists of the cochlea and several non-auditory structures. The cochlea is lined with hair cells which transform the fluid waves of sound into nerve signals that are carried along the neural pathways of the central auditory nervous system that extends

from the brain stem to the temporal lobes of the cerebral cortex of the brain.

As the auditory information (sound) travels through the neural system, it is "processed," allowing the listener to determine the direction from which the sound came, identify the type of sound, separate the sound from background noise, interpret the sound, and store it for future retrieval from long- and short-term memory.

The Visual System

The visual sensory system is designed to focus, detect, transmit and interpret what is seen; the ocular motor system is designed to keep the two eyes aligned with each other and aimed at the target of interest. Stated more simply, the visual sensory system is composed of binocular functions and ocular motility. Binocular function refers to the ability of the eyes to work together properly, coordinating their activity so both eyes focus on the same object, and the ability of the eyes to shift their focus from near to far distance points easily and effortlessly. Ocular motility or tracking refers to the ability of the eyes to move together across a page of print, to follow a moving object in space, or to move together from one viewing area to another.

A change in either the ability of the eyes to work together or eye movement will signal a similar change in the function of the other. What needs to be understood is that vision is more than just 20/20 vision. It also includes binocular coordination, speed accommodation, vertical movement and other visual functions necessary to see, understand and apply the information that comes through the eyes.

What Does This Mean for My Child?

As children develop, the neurological pathways in the brain increase, allowing the child to handle larger amounts of sensory information. The proper development of these systems is dependent upon active movement and exercise during the corresponding growth periods. When children are subjected to abuse or neglect or do not have the opportunity to do activities that correspond with each stage of development, their neurological systems will not fully mature. Necessary activities include crawling, walking, hearing sound (preferably the human voice), looking at faces, touching things, crawling, picking up small objects, walking upright, running, swinging arms, hopping, skipping, jumping and other activities that require coordination and balance.

Sensory input, motor activities and nurturing develop the proper sequence of neurological development essential for learning. Neural development is a process which must be accompanied by motor functioning. If motor input (exercise) is nonexistent, limited or confused, the sensory pathways will not develop completely. If for some reason neurological development is delayed, the child may benefit from therapy comprised of activities and sensory experiences that have proven beneficial in promoting neurological organization. These experiences may begin with activities characteristic of early infancy and progress through the various stages of growth.

Physical trauma is another factor that contributes to processing problems. If for some reason the child experiences trauma to the head or spine, care should be taken to evaluate the nature of the injury and seek professional help when needed. In many cases, after a significant head or spinal trauma, the child will complain of headaches, neck or back pain. While these injuries will self-resolve in time, they still can be the trigger for diminished visual and auditory abilities.

Injuries to the back of the head can interfere with the visual centers located at the back of the brain. These traumas may manifest themselves as visual acuity problems or altered eye tracking and teaming problems, which will impact reading. A vision exam may find 20/20 visual clarity, but what may also be evident is that the child now sees two books instead of one, or the book is blurred and he may not see it clearly enough to read it, or he may only see the center of the page and not the information at the beginning or end of the line of print and, most commonly, he will not be able to read fluently.

The following case study is an example of the impact of physical injury on the visual and vestibular systems. Immature neurological development is discussed the next chapter.

Case Study

A young male second-grade student was referred for assessment to determine eligibility for special education. Initial investigation revealed that he could not read fluently, although it appeared that he could read the words in isolation. Further, he could not keep the numbers properly aligned in mathematics in order to come up with the correct answer in the addition and subtraction of numbers. The answer to the problem as he wrote it was correct, but it was not the right problem so he did not receive credit.

Assessment revealed high-average intelligence, the presence of a visual processing problem and a discrepancy between ability and achievement. An eye tracking test revealed that he could not move his eyeballs in either direction, and that he had to turn his head in order to follow a moving object.

In talking with the child, he revealed that while riding on his skate board he had run into a telephone pole and that he had hit the pole so hard that he didn't remember much else. He was told by some friends that they had found him lying on the street and had taken him home, where he was put into bed. Three days later when he got up, his parents sent him back to school.

The child stated that when he returned to school, he was not able to see as well and couldn't read anymore and sometimes it was also hard to hear. A concussion is a likely candidate as the cause of the problems, but he had received no medical attention.

What to Do

Now, the reasoning should be that if the child had an accident and the resulting trauma to his head or spine interfered with function of the visual and auditory systems, the treatment should be a visit to a good professional with knowledge of treatment of processing disorders, not "special education." Remember, the primary responsibility of the school is to educate the child, and their only response to disabled or injured children is to place them in special education. School districts do not always take responsibility for assisting parents in getting the proper medical care for their children.

An Exercise to Do at Home

Eye muscle control can be checked at home using these simple steps (this makes a good eye training exercise also):

1.   Have the child focus on a finger held about 12 inches in front of his eyes.

2.   Ask the child to follow your finger with his eyes without moving his head.

3.   Always keep the finger the same 12 inches from his face.

4.   Begin at the midline (in front of his nose) and slowly move to the right side.

5.   Next, start at the midline and slowly move the finger to the left.

6.   Carefully observe how smoothly the child is able to move his eyes.

7.   If the eyes jerk back or he loses focus, just start over.

8.   Next, begin the exercise with the finger on the far right side and bring it back toward the middle and on to the left side.

9.   Pay special attention to what happens when the finger crosses in front of the nose. Does the child lose focus; do the eyes jump or wobble back and forth?

The eyes should move smoothly from one side of the body, across the midline to the other side without difficulty. Avoidance of the task suggests that the exercise is difficult or uncomfortable. Check with the classroom teacher to see how fluently the child reads or listen to him read at home. If reading is a problem, it may be time for a professional evaluation. It should be noted that simple accidents which cause trauma to the head or spine will eventually lead to more serious problems if not corrected.

CHAPTER III

IMMATURE DEVELOPMENT

Developmental readiness refers to children's overall ability to adapt to the challenges of school. By the age of five, when children enter kindergarten, they are assumed to have reached a level of maturation at which they will be able to learn, write letters and numbers and to interact socially with other children. When a child cannot do these things, he is considered to be developmentally immature.

Immature development is a common cause of school problems in kindergarten and first-grade children. The brain and central nervous system are again involved, but without dysfunction. This time, the entire central nervous system and all its subsystems have not matured as completely in one child as in another. While the child is likely to "catch up" later, the problem is the intervening years of school failure while the nervous system remains immature.

If an immature child attends pre-school, it is likely that the teacher will point out that he is not ready for kindergarten. An evaluation by a professional should be sought to confirm this information. If the finding is true, it is usually accompanied by a recommendation that the child not enter kindergarten for another year so that he will have time to mature to a level of "readiness" to learn.

Often when this advice is not heeded by parents, it turns out to be a tragic decision. By the time these children achieve the perceptual motor development of their classmates, usually by third grade, they have lost three years of instruction. The lessons from kindergarten and first grade are not repeated in second or third grade, and the child is unsuccessful because he has not acquired the basic knowledge and skills upon which third grade instruction is built.

Assessment may reveal the presence of immature visual processing, auditory processing or immature visual-motor skills. All of these will contribute to a determination of eligibility for special education.

How Did This Happen?

As development takes place in the womb, the nervous system develops first and should develop through several stages. Therefore, premature birth is the first place to look for causes of immature development. However, even children of full-term deliveries will present as developmentally immature if there is limited opportunity for physical activity.

Otherwise healthy children present with developmental immaturity when they have had limited opportunity for the physical exercise needed to bring about an integration of the neural pathways in the central nervous system. Without sufficient exercise, the physical body and central nervous system do not develop and higher cognitive functions never integrate. It has long been the practice of families with children to move into a house with a large backyard so that children will have a place to play. The greater benefit is that the opportunity for gross motor play will produce healthier, more well developed children.

What to Do

If developmental "unreadiness" is the diagnosis when the child enters school, the ideal situation would be to delay entry into kindergarten for one year or have the child enjoy a second year of kindergarten. During the second year he will be mature enough to learn the lessons and the advantage of prior learning may make him an outstanding student.   When one has an older child who was not developmentally ready and is now struggling, this is a time to accept enrollment in special education so that he can get the individualized help needed to make up for the years when learning did not take place. However, you must remain an advocate to insure that areas of specific weakness are being addressed and that the program is designed to develop those skills not learned in earlier grades.

The Individual Education Plan (IEP) should not be a support system for the work in his present grade. There should be a statement of identified areas of weakness with instructional strategies designed to encourage improvement in the identified areas. Periodic checks should be made to measure improvement. If improvement is not occurring, the IEP should be redesigned.

Treatment to address this immaturity is easy and very effective. It can be done professionally, or it can be done easily at home. Increased physical exercise with cross crawl experiences similar to those of learning to crawl during normal development builds the early reflexes and lays the foundation for more mature development.

Follow this with plenty of physical activity of the sort that a child gets by running and playing outside. Common activities include rolling, jumping, hopping, skipping, crawling and balancing on one foot on a "2x4" raised about 2 inches above the ground. The curb at the side of the street is also effective for balancing. And most cities have large parks with jungle gyms and other climbing apparatus.

And it's never too late for lots of physical activity in a big back yard, park, gym, YMCA or on a soccer or baseball team.

All these activities will lay a foundation for fine-tuning intellectual, physical and emotional systems.

Case Studies

A five-year-old female child at kindergarten pre-registration presented with the physical development of a three-year-old. However, the size of her head and cranium appeared to be normal and she exhibited average intelligence.

During observation, walking appeared to be a challenge for her and going up and down stairs seemed especially difficult. Upon inquiry the parents revealed that they lived in a high- rise condominium in a large city and that they both worked. Because of the city environment, the child was not allowed to go outside alone because a great deal of time and effort was required by her parents to accompany her outside to play. As a consequence, the only time that the child had spent out-of-doors was while riding in the car. She had spent her whole five years with the companionship of the television. Language development occurred through interaction with the TV. She had learned all the songs, letters and numbers offered by children's programs and had gained insights from other programming.

Because of her advanced cognitive development, she was permitted to enter kindergarten; however, her physical development presented problems. Recommendations included instructions to the parents to secure special physical exercise and training for the child. Interventions at school included having an upper-level child accompany her on a walk two times a day around the perimeter of the school playground. Unfortunately, there were only three steps in the whole school, so she was told to climb the three steps on each trip through the building and around the playground.

A five-year-old male, upon entry into kindergarten, exhibited with an even lower level of physical and intellectual development. He was so small in stature that he was still wearing the high lace-up shoes characteristic of training shoes.

In this case the child lived in a neighborhood with both sets of grandparents. During registration, the parents and both sets of grandparents were present. For the thirty minutes of the interview, the child's feet never touched the ground. When the parents were required to sign something, they handed him to a grandparent. When that grandparent attempted to put him down, the other grandparent picked him up.

Upon inquiry about the child's immature level of development, one of the grandparents explained that the child's feet had never touched the ground—an adult was always ready to take a turn holding him. And surprisingly, the soles of the child's shoes were not scuffed. They still had the shiny surface of a new pair of shoes.

This child was denied admission to kindergarten because of limited potential for success. A program of physical activity was recommended and the child was referred to his family pediatrician.

When Retention Has Been Recommended[ii]

There are many reasons why children fail in the classroom. And in some circumstances retention may help. However, after kindergarten most classroom failure will not be solved when a child repeats a grade. In fact, studies show that most cases of retention are unsuccessful and the child is usually hurt by it. The child's academic progress is delayed, the child loses his or her peer group and the child feels he or she has been labeled "stupid" or "a failure." The child then feels totally useless when he or she is no more successful the second time through a grade and is placed in special education.

One can see how important it is to thoroughly investigate the cause of school failure before acting on a retention recommendation. All the following jobs should be completed before agreeing to retention or special education.

The child's classroom teacher should clearly document the skills that the child has not mastered during the current school year. For example, for a kindergarten child this documentation could show that the child has not learned to identify all the letters in the alphabet, does not grasp simple concepts or cannot follow directions and work independently. A fourth- grade teacher might show that the child cannot yet solve the math problems in the fourth grade workbook at an acceptable level and in more than one subject area cannot grasp the concepts being presented.

The teacher of the next grade level should review these deficits and decide whether the child could learn the lessons to be taught in the next grade. There are times when a child can do poorly in one grade and yet "catch up" with classmates during the next year. Sometimes teachers re-teach lessons from the previous grade and might not expect full mastery of all lessons. However, this can be known only if the current teacher consults with the teacher of the next grade level about the next year's lesson plan.

If the first two steps indicate a problem for the child in the next year, then parents should confer with the current teacher and perhaps also with the school principal. In this meeting plans for a formal assessment should begin. A formal assessment includes intelligence and achievement testing, teacher, child and parent interviews and screening for emotional disorders.

The child should be referred to a school psychologist or to an independent psychologist with training in school psychology. Specific learning strengths and weaknesses needed to do instructional planning and design classroom intervention should be assessed using an instrument like the Cognitive Assessment System (CAS). The CAS is fully explained in Chapter XII Tests and Testing.

This decision should be made by the student study team, made up of the parent, the present classroom teacher, next year's teacher and a school administrator, at a minimum. If the school team concludes that an outside assessment by a professional other than a school employee is needed, the school district is required to pay for it. However, the child's parents must give written permission in the form of their signature on a written Assessment Plan. Under "other" on the school's form, insert the additional outside evaluation if there is agreement on the need. This is also where you would list a preference for the use of the Cognitive Assessment System, if it is not already listed as an option.

Finally, all the parties in the evaluation process meet for a final planning session.   In the planning session, all the pertinent information about the child is available and the cause of the child's school failure is discussed. This meeting gives everyone an opportunity to make a joint decision about the best solution to the school failure. In some cases, kindergarten retention alone can give the child the solid basis for better learning in the future.

Children with learning disabilities need specialized education and under the law they are protected from being retained. Retention should not be considered for any child without a thorough evaluation of strengths and weaknesses, the designing of an instructional plan and the development of interventions for the general education classroom. Retention alone is not recommended for any child and you should accept retention only when all the above steps have been completed. Even then, you should continue to monitor the next year to be certain that your child's intervention plan is being followed.

CHAPTER IV

PARENTING

Parenting is considered by many to be the singular most important form of human interaction. Technically, parenting is a process of interactions designed to nourish, protect and guide a new life through the course of its development. The process of parenting entails four main tasks:

- To foster physical and mental health
- To provide emotional warmth and nurturing
- To provide opportunities for the development of individuality and intellect, and
- To facilitate social and emotional competence.

Parenting begins with the process of establishing an unconditional positive regard and acceptance of the child, known as bonding. Attachment describes an extension of bonding; it is that close relationship that develops between parent and child, which continues throughout life. It is through these relationships that the child is nurtured into mature physical, emotional and psychological development.

Research on a number of levels suggests that what parents do, or do not do, has profound impact upon how the child's mind develops. Surprisingly, research has verified the significant impact that experiences of a primarily social nature have upon the development of the central nervous system.

These studies support the fact that when an adult provides a secure attachment to a child involving a sense of safety and protection, it allows the child's mind to develop a rich, intricate and complex set of interconnections among different aspects of the brain.

At birth the human brain is undeveloped. It is during childhood that the brain matures and a whole set of brain-related capabilities develop in a sequential fashion (we crawl before we walk, we babble before we talk).

The process of sequential development of the brain is guided by experience. As different regions of the brain are organizing, they require specific kinds of experiences targeting that region's specific function (e.g., visual input while the visual system is organizing) in order to develop normally. These times during development are called critical or sensitive periods.

For millions of abused and neglected children, the nature of their experience adversely influences the development of their brain. All relationships, especially primary relationships, profoundly impact the developing brain, for better or worse. When children feel validated, safe and supported, their nervous system develops in a very coherent manner; but if they don't feel safe and connected in their primary relationships, their brain develops in a disrupted way.

Why Does This Happen?

World War II changed the world and with it, the meaning of family in the United States. Prior to the war, most Americans lived in small towns with aunts, uncles and grandparents close by, and divorce was rare. After the war most people, especially young families, moved to cities and suburbs. As a result of this separation, the precious connection that comes with belonging to a supportive community and being mentored by close relatives and friends was lost.

Real parent education took place in these intimate relationships that disappeared after the war. Young women having babies have no experienced parent figure to assist them with the challenges of child-rearing. The consequence of young mothers with no practical experience of their own and no experienced grandparent to teach childrearing has had a negative impact upon two generations of children.

Aid for Dependent Children was instituted shortly after WWII to assist the mothers and children whose husbands and fathers were killed in the war. The objective of the program was to insure that every child had at least one parent at home. It was thought that children with at least one parent at home would insure the future of the nation. However, providing money alone failed to address the problem. There needed to be training, support and a nurturing family in which to rear children.

The brain is shaped by the environment, and it is the environment within the home that most impacts the development of a child. Many learning disabilities occur because the family as it is presently constituted does not have the available resources to accomplish identified ideal childrearing objectives, and there is no substitute.

Efforts to meet these challenges have not been successful. There are 45,000 licensed childcare centers in California alone. Fewer than 15 percent nationally are of high quality and even the best—with four babies per caregiver—"deprive children of the regular emotional nurturance necessary for healthy development."[iv]

Unfortunately, efforts to meet the emotional and psychological needs of abusive or negligent parents have been equally unsuccessful. Unfortunately for a growing number of children, the most significant period of growth from birth to age three has become a time of abuse, neglect, stress, violence and little or no stimulation. Each year in the United States alone, over three million children are abused or neglected. And unless there is neurological damage from the abuse, neglect has a longer-term, more damaging impact on the development of the child.

The consequences of the lack of nurturing are severe. Harvard University researchers have identified four permanent brain abnormalities caused by a lack of nurturing, early abuse and neglect. Suicide is the third-leading cause of death of American children ages five to fifteen and the prevalence of learning disabilities increases by 10 to 20 percent every 10 years

What Does This Mean for My Child?

Beginning in infancy and early childhood, trauma to either the child or principal caretaker may interfere with early emotional developmental processes. Fortunately, the hope for these children is that all forms of trauma, including relational trauma and single-incident trauma, can be readily repaired. Early childhood trauma changes the biology of the brain, but early childhood support also changes the biology of the brain. Even when a child has a poor relationship with a primary caretaker, if that child has as few as one secure relationship with another adult, childcare or daycare provider, there is hope for healing the brain. Children who recover from emotional trauma are those who have other human beings who are kind, patient, sensitive and supportive.

What to Do

Seek out some help with child-rearing. Call your mother, aunt, older sister or the lady across the street. Do their children have learning disabilities? Read something, ask somebody or email this author or anyone in the list of references throughout this book. You are not in this alone. There is lots of help available from professional organizations, retired teachers, Big Brothers/Big Sisters, mentoring programs, Boys/Girls Club, YMCA, YWCA and community centers. All these places have help or know where to find it. Remember, it takes only one caring adult who interacts with the child in a meaningful way.

"Quality versus quantity" is the old argument of how you spend the time that you do have available to spend with your child. If you don't have a lot of time, put some quality into the time that you do have. If you have only two hours per day to devote to your child, don't spend it in front of the television set, do something of quality, play a board game, read a story, talk about school, take a walk around the block, or go to the park and play, not to the movies. Your child wants and needs your full attention.

Good nurturing means human contact. For infants and growing children, this means physical contact as well: holding, rocking, playing together, "rough housing" (I think that means wrestling indoors). Ride him on your back or in front in a sling and mostly give your full attention and involvement.

Evidence suggests that there is something significant in human contact and demonstrated affection between parent and child. The fact that within 18 months children fail to thrive and/or die without it, certainly suggests that it plays a major role in child development. Permanent brain damage resulting from neglect and abuse suggests another connection. We humans are spiritual beings and cannot live without at least one meaningful connection with another caring, involved spiritual human being. Our very lives depend upon it.

CHAPTER V

EMOTIONAL TRAUMA

Even when a child survives childhood development with parental bonding and attachments intact, emotional trauma can have a significant impact. A traumatic event is one that causes you, your child or your family a great deal of pain. Trauma results from events like:

- Natural disasters (earthquakes, fires, floods, hurricanes, etc.)
- Physical assault, including rape, incest, molestation, domestic abuse (hearing parents arguing and fighting over a period of time)
- Serious bodily harm (brutal whippings or beatings)
- Serious accidents such as automobile or other high-impact scenarios
- Experiencing or witnessing horrific injury, carnage or fatalities, as in war or inner-city gang wars and drive-by shooting[v]

Unfortunately, children comprise the largest group of victims of these traumatic experiences. Each year in the United States alone, it is estimated that more than 5 million children are traumatized in some way. Taken together, a conservative estimate of children currently at risk exceeds 15 million, and grows as traumatized children carry their scars into adulthood and new children are traumatized each year.[vi]

What does this mean for my child?

Because of the development of brain scan technology, scientists can now observe the brain in action without waiting for an autopsy. These scans reveal that emotional trauma actually changes the structure and function of the brain at the point where the frontal cortex, the emotional brain and the survival brain converge; thereby, having a significant impact upon emotional, behavioral, cognitive, social and physical development of children. [vii]

These changes in the brain may diminish the concentration, organizational ability and language skills that children need for school. Additionally, they may manifest as hyperactivity, inattention, inability to concentrate, inability to conceptualize and poor memory. If a child who has been traumatized remains in an aroused state of fear and finds it difficult to process verbal information, it then becomes difficult to follow directions, to recall what was heard and to make sense out of what is being said. Focusing, attending, retaining and recalling verbal information becomes very difficult. These language problems can undermine literacy skills, social-emotional development and behavioral self-control.[viii]

Fortunately, children exposed to this same traumatic event react differently. Some will develop severe psychological distress while others will not.[ix] For those that do develop symptoms, beginning in fancy and early childhood, trauma to either the child or principal caretaker may interfere with early development of emotional processes. Infants sensitive to caretakers' emotional state and behavior may respond with disturbances of excessive crying, eating, sleep or apathy and failure to thrive.

Toddlers add to these symptoms a tendency to become more dependent and clingy, ore active physically and aggressive. Preschoolers add complaints of pain without injury, avoidance, fears and/or sadness and may show delays in cognition, including language development, or present as withdrawn and mute. Their aggressiveness and vengefulness may be erroneously labeled as a behavior disorder.

In addition, school-age children may be anxious, depressed or inhibited and may report guilt, change in play, loss of or change interests, return of old or onset of new fears, sleep disorders and impaired concentration, functioning and initiative. They may also manifest disorders in school performance and learning.

Adolescents may add problems with personal identity, personality disorders, and pseudo-seizures. They may become suicidal and act out sexually. Substance abuse, delinquency, truancy and academic failure have also been noted. [ix]

Child development psychologists have explored the question of why many children experience trauma and remain competent even under adverse conditions such as exposure to domestic violence, abuse, homelessness, war and community violence. They found three key factors common to all competent children, whether or not they grow up in favorable circumstances:

- a strong parent-child relationship, or, when such a relationship is not available, a surrogate care-giving figure who serves a mentoring role;
- good cognitive skills that predict academic success and lead to rule-abiding behavior; and
- the ability to self-regulate attention, emotions and behavior. [x]

Researchers explain that poverty, chronic stress, domestic violence, natural disasters, and other high-risk contexts for child development may have lasting effects when they damage or impair one of these three crucial adaptive systems. However, by the same token, they point out that bolstering these three key factors can help children succeed. Studies show that it is never too late to create positive change in a child's life, or in an adult's, for that matter. Studies have shown that the learning that accompanies new experiences can alter the damaged neural connections in the brain.

Relationships with relatives, teachers and childcare providers can provide an important source of connection and strength for the child's developing mind. The older a is, the harder this will be, but children never lose their need for emotional connection with their primary caretaker, so opportunity for repair remains open.

Repair is nurtured by experiences that feel safe, that are playful and fun for all, allow for differences and respect individuality. [xi]

What to Do

There are several things that parents and others who care for children can do to help alleviate the emotional consequences of trauma. Spend more time with children and let them be more dependent on you during the months following the trauma; for example, allowing your child to cling to you more often than usual. Physical affection is very comforting to children who have experienced trauma.

Provide play experiences to help relieve tension. Younger children in particular may find it easier to share their ideas and feelings about the event through non-verbal activities such as drawing.

Encourage older children to speak with you and with one another about their thoughts and feelings. This helps reduce their confusion and anxiety related to the trauma. Respond to questions in terms they can comprehend. Reassure them repeatedly that you care about them and that you understand their fears and concerns.

Keep regular schedules for activities such as eating, playing and going to bed to help restore a sense of security and normalcy.[xii]

Also, validating the child by giving him/her your time is important. Be available when you are at home. Listen when he tries to talk to you, allowing him to communicate his feelings. Just listen and don't ask a lot of questions, find fault, teach, or give instructions. Just listen as you would listen to another adult. You can become emotional later in private. Don't let him know that what he said was upsetting to you, and don't tell him that you don't believe what he is saying. If you get angry or show emotion while he is telling you the horror story about what someone id to him sexually he will stop talking and you may never learn that it also was or is being done to his little brother or big sister and perhaps all the other children in the neighborhood by the pedophile who lives on the block, or "uncle" Joe who drops by on occasion. In addition to that, he will not tell you anything else, because he can't trust that you are mature enough to handle certain kinds of information or that "they won't believe me anyway."

Emotional trauma impacts learning, but special education is not the only answer. There is a need to address the traumatic memories that your child carriers. Those traumatic memories will remain for the rest of his life, so learning is not the only factor involved. His future as a student, spouse and parent all depend upon what you do with his emotional trauma now.

It may be necessary to get professional help. Before you take the appointment, however, you can begin collecting information about your child's experiences and make an educated guess about the source of the trauma. You know whether he has been in a natural disaster such as a floor or tornado. You also know if he has been sexually assaulted, abused or neglected. And, most overlooked, is the fighting and arguing between spouses which led up to a nasty divorce and the child was separated from his parents for a long period of time while he stayed with a grandparent.

If there are things like this in your child's emotional history, be honest with yourself, document as much as possible, prepare to discuss it with the therapist you plan to see and then brainstorm some more when you get there.

Again, the kindest, most loving contribution you can make to this effort is to begin to nurture the child on a regular basis. Build it into your schedule of activities. Hugs, kisses, kind words and attention from his parents are assurances that he is loved. Being tucked into bed and assured that all is well will work wonders as the child recovers from trauma.

While emotional trauma does not negatively affect the learning of all children, studies show that children who are abused or otherwise traumatized are more likely be in special education, have below-grade-level achievement test scores, have poor work habits and are 2.5 times more likely to fail a grade.

What the Schools Might Do[xii]

When evaluating a student for special education it is important to consider the possibility that trauma may be laying a role, as it is easy to inadvertently misdiagnose some of the trauma-related symptoms.

Traumatized children are often misdiagnosed and inappropriately placed, because many of the learning problems associated with trauma are identified by the Disabilities Education Act of 1977 as a learning disability, and the primary behavioral characteristics of trauma re identified as Emotional Disturbance, and the child who exhibits the behavioral characteristics of trauma are identified as Emotionally Disturbed, and the child who exhibits the behavioral characteristics of trauma is labeled ADD or ADHD. Clinical research seems to suggest that they are all one and the same. Each label seems to be describing a different facet of the same disorder.

It may be time to redefine learning disabilities and acknowledge that in some incidences it is well known what causes learning disabilities, and having acknowledged the cause, we may begin an "appropriate" approach to the problem. This would require broadening the role and function of special education, eligibility for services and above all, expansion of the role, function and knowledge base of the school psychologist. Simply determining eligibility for special education is not a worthwhile role for such a highly trained and highly compensated professional.

With the help of educators, traumatized children can flourish in their school communities and master the educational tasks of childhood despite their overwhelmingly stressful experiences. This requires a school environment that supports both staff and children and that recognizes and responds to the effects that childhood trauma can have on children's learning and behavior.

Wile school have the mission of educating children, it may become necessary for the schools, in order to accomplish the mission of educating children, may have to take an active role in seeing that the responsibility for addressing the consequences of trauma that interfered with learning is mandated to some other publicly funded entity. The new public law No Child Left Behind mandates that these children receive a free, appropriate, public education. Therefore, schools have a responsibility for educating them, and may need to assume a role in assuring that they are ready to be education.

The increase in trauma experienced by children is a consequence of the changes in the society in which they live. Should not the society then assume responsibility for protecting itself from the consequences of its own irresponsibility by at least partnering with therapeutic programming to be offered within or in close proximity to the school environment?

CHAPTER VI

NUTRITION, ALLERGIES AND HYPOGLYCEMIA

Another in a wide array of important factors for brain development and intellectual capacity appears to be a child's daily nutrition. The nutritional habits followed by most people today, especially children, present significant obstacles to learning. It may be accurate to say that the diet of most American children today is a diet that automatically results in a very low level of intelligence. The U.S. Department of Agriculture states that only two percent of children actually meet the recommendations of the Food Guide Pyramid, resulting in a lack of sufficient nutrients to build a healthy brain and nervous system in 98% of our children.[iii][iv]

Making matters worse, most Americans simply don't eat enough of the critical nutrients needed to build and maintain the brain from infancy. We begin by depriving our children of GLA (gamma linolenic acid), an essential fatty acid found in abundance in human breast milk, but entirely missing from cow's milk. Not surprisingly, clinical studies have shown that babies weaned on cow's milk score lower on intelligence tests than those weaned on human breast milk.

Malnutrition, both before and during the first few years after birth, has been shown to result in stunted brain growth and slower passage of electrical signals in the brain, because hungry children are less likely to interact with other people or explore or learn from their surroundings. This interferes with their ability to learn from a very early age.

New research shows that even mild under-nutrition can prevent learning. The human brain is a delicate organ; it requires a precise mixture of water, blood sugar, temperature, electrolyte minerals, essential fatty acids and a whole host of other nutrients to function correctly. Alter even one of these just slightly and brain function suffers dramatically. These effects on the brain are linked to cognitive, social and behavioral deficits with possible long-term consequences.

Iron-deficiency anemia, the most common form of malnutrition in the United States, can result in cognitive and motor delays, anxiety, depression, social problems and problems with attention. Protein deficiency can result in motor and cognitive delays and impulsive behavior.

The brain has a greater percentage of fat than any other organ in the body; 20% of the dry weight of the brain is comprised of essential fatty acids. The possible deficiency in a child of what is termed essential fatty acids (EFAs) frequently interferes with a child's ability to cope with the demands of school. If a child does not get enough EFAs, the myelin sheath protecting the axons of billions of nerve cells may not be adequate. Recent research is showing that boys with ADD have EFA deficiencies and similar deficiencies are possibly responsible for the symptoms of many forms of dyslexia.

Like vitamins, essential fatty acids cannot be produced by the body; they have to come from the food we eat. The fact that our diets have deteriorated over the past years increases the possibility of EFA deficiency. Previously, animals hunted by man were free-ranging, grazed off natural grasslands and had much higher levels of Omega-3 EFA than domesticated animals. Today much of our farmed meat supply (chicken, beef and pork) is fed on large amounts of corn and soybean meal that contain Omega-6 EFAs, but little or no Omega-3 EFAs. This is the reason for the recent interest in free-range meats and eggs from free-range chickens, as well as supplementation with Omega-3 EFAs.

Beyond the lack of essential nutrients found in the American diet, the brain function of children is especially susceptible to the influence of destructive dietary ingredients such as refined white flour, white sugar, high-fructose corn syrup (the primary sweetener in soft drinks) and caffeine. The average Western child's diet is almost a prescription for a deficiency of glucose (sugar) in the blood, called hypoglycemia.[v]

The two most significant factors contributing to hypoglycemia are diet and emotional stress. Common foods like white bread, sugar and fizzy drinks contain refined carbohydrates, which absorb very rapidly into the bloodstream because little digestion is required. These foods cause a rapid increase in blood sugar levels, followed by an increase in the production of insulin, which removes sugar from the blood and results in a low level of blood sugar.

Complex carbohydrates, found in vegetables and whole grains, help to avoid hypoglycemia by replenishing glucose at regular intervals. These foods take longer to digest, releasing nutrients into the blood stream gradually. This keeps the body's energy constant.

In a large-scale study, 200 hyperactive children had low blood sugar often enough that it started or aggravated typical hyperactive behavior. Many of these children also had allergies to common foods. These were usually the foods that they favored and ate whenever possible. This set off abnormal behaviors, many of which were the same ones found to be characteristic of underachieving children.

In another study with 265 hyperactive children, it was found that glucose tolerance tests were abnormal in 76%. This suggests that abnormal glucose metabolism may be a factor in the cause of hyperactivity. These studies in the UK with so-called hyperactive children have demonstrated quite convincingly—change the child's diet and the behavior shifts in a matter of days.[vi]

A hypoglycemic child often needs to eat every hour or two during school hours as well as at home in order to avoid low blood sugar reactions, which cause recurrent fatigue, irritability, tension, hyperactivity and aggression.

Some forms of hyperactivity, short attention span and mood swings are caused by allergies and intolerances for certain foods and other environmental factors.[vii] Allergies can also play havoc with a child's ability to benefit from teaching. There is much controversy in the medical and related fields concerning allergies and their identification. Because allergies are difficult to research, little is known about allergies and they are seldom mentioned or tested for by doctors.[viii]

Image

Impact of allergies on the drawings of a 6 year old boy

Some of what is known about allergies is that they have a significant impact upon a child's performance. Above is a drawing made by a six–year-old boy before he at a breakfast of toast, apple juice, egg and butter. He continued to draw every few minutes over the next half hour. You can see the

gradual deterioration in his drawings. Imagine how difficult it would be for him to learn each school day if this were his routine breakfast. It is important to investigate whether food packed for his school snack could produce similar changes.

Image

Impact of Allergies on Robert's Handwriting

When 4½-year-old Robert was allergy-tested for oats and wheat his handwriting and behavior changed at the same time. For these reasons, when a child is diagnosed with learning problems and poor behavior, consideration should be given to the role that chemicals, stress, food allergies and other factors in the environment may be having upon the child's performance. A change in his diet and some experimentation to find the source of stress or what might be causing allergies seems more logical. Behavior modification, counseling and medications to which he may also be allergic are not appropriate therapies for allergies, hypoglycemia and stress.

What Does This Mean for My Child

If you are eating an unhealthy diet, then you are cheating yourself out of you brain's full potential. But even worse, by preparing a poor diet, you're dooming your children to a future of mediocre intelligence, poor eyesight, decreased hearing, delayed and deficient verbal skills and more.

The modern habit of eating fast foods means that many children (and adults) are not eating enough of the omega-3

EFAs that the brain needs to function properly. And this is made worse by the fact that we eat too much of the omega-6 fats in manufactured and fried foods, which block the production of DHA and EPA from a natural, original food source. So by feeding our children fast foods, they are not only getting less of the good fats in their diet, they are also greatly diminishing the value of the good fats that they do consume. This can severely damage brain development and functioning.

What to Do

Take a long, serious look at your child. Obvious changes sometimes occur in the behavior and physical appearance of children and adults who have typical allergies or food or chemical sensitivities.

Allergies to environmental chemical odors such as perfume or certain cleaning materials, tend to occur within seconds or a very few minutes. Food reactions take fifteen to sixty minutes to become apparent. A reaction to dust or molds usually occurs within an hour. Parents can often pinpoint the cause merely by thinking back over what happened. For example, if red earlobes, a severe headache, or wiggly legs occur half an hour after lunch, it would be logical to assume the symptoms are possibly related to something that was eaten.

One clue in spotting hypoglycemia is the way young children ask for food. Do they request food or demand it? The later suggests low blood sugar. It can happen on and off all day, but it is most apt to occur between 10:30 and 11:30 a.m. and again between 3:00 and 4:00 p.m. Other symptoms of hypoglycemia include an inability to concentrate, mood swings, anxiety, depression and being more emotional than usual. Asthma, fatigue, headache, nervousness, insomnia, irritability, restlessness, poor memory and indecisiveness are also frequently reported.

Parents should learn to watch for dark eye circles (which can be black, blue or pink), red earlobes (sometimes becoming so hot that ice is needed to provide relief), nose-rubbing, skin-scratching, wiggly legs, yawning and various throaty sounds. Small, horizontal wrinkles under the eyes are typical of allergic children, especially those who have eczema.

Sudden unprovoked aggression in both children and adults can be related to allergy. It is often associated with red earlobes, wiggly legs, dark eye circles and a special, abnormal spaced out 'look.' Behavior may include hitting, biting, kicking, spitting and punching.

Other food allergies can be recognized by paying attention to what your child eats or asks for most often. If there is a change in behavior, headache or other discomfort after eating these foods, suspect that there is an allergy involved. If he craves soft drinks and other caffeinated beverages, you might suspect hypoglycemia and replace the soft drinks with water or replace the sugar-coated cereal with more whole grain foods.

Remember that some nationalities and ethnic groups are allergic to wheat and some have an allergy to milk. African-American children exhibit allergies to chocolate and sometimes as often to wheat, so you may have to experiment with careful attention to changes in appearance and behavior after your child has eaten those foods.

If the problem is eczema, watch the arm and leg creases; these areas commonly become red and itchy during meals or immediately after contact with dust, molds, or certain foods. The actual rash, however, will not develop until the next day. Also suspect food allergies if your child has any form of intestinal complaints after eating. If dark eye circles and muscle aches routinely occur after gym, art, chemistry or biology class or after a shower, suspect a reaction to chemical exposure.

If these changes occur after play on freshly cut grass, suspect grass pollen. If a child's nose becomes itchy and drippy or if asthma and coughing get worse after tumbling on gym mats or playing on an old carpet, the cause could be dust, molds, or both. If a youngster becomes wild and uncontrollable and has a peculiar spaced-out look after using a bathroom that smells of scented body preparations, deodorants or disinfectants, suspect chemicals.

Remember, your child is a total organism. All parts must work optimally at all times. If one part becomes deficient, the whole system is affected. The best advice for those interested in seeing that their child's abilities are at their peak is to see that he gets plenty of exercise, adequate sleep, good nutrition, takes frequent breaks to recharge his psychological batteries and eats a wide variety of foods to provide needed essential minerals and drink plenty of water.[ix]

And before accepting a label of learning problems and poor

behavior, insist upon finding out what role chemicals, food and other environmental factors may be playing in the behavioral changes.

Vary the menu to include foods you don't frequently eat. Fruits and vegetables should be eaten at every meal. The vitamins and minerals work even if you don't like the vegetables. You don't have to be a gourmet chef to feed kids. And, guess what? Kids will eat what they are taught to eat. Set some standards for meals and encourage kids to try new things. Don't punish with "you have to eat all your vegetables before you leave the table." Let them leave when they think they are finished. When they come back later and ask for a snack, provide a nutritious one like an apple, orange, banana, pumpkin seeds, sunflower seeds or dried fruit.

Children who eat healthful foods will be more likely to choose healthful foods for a lifetime. Children weaned on dates, raisins and other dried fruit actually learn to like the taste. Children do not crave what they have never experienced and tastes can be changed.

Unfortunately, studies show that overweight children tend to become overweight adults. Teach your children about healthful foods. Read over the different food pyramids and have your kids pick out some favorite foods from each food group. Have them help you plan a meal that includes a healthy serving of protein, a vegetable or two, and a healthful fruit for dessert. For young kids, make a chart to keep track of all the fruits and vegetables they eat (we need at least five servings of fruits and veggies every day).[x]

The best way to avoid hypoglycemia and behavioral problems in school-age children is to be sure that they eat a nutritious breakfast. As with other meals, breakfast should include a variety of foods, including:

- grains (breads and cereals)
- protein (meats, beans, and nuts)
- fruits and vegetables
- milk, cheese, and yogurt

When breakfast has to be skipped because of sleeping too late or it is thought to be a way to stay thin, try these quick breakfasts. They're easy to grab on the way out the door or can be prepared the night before.

- fresh fruit
- whole-grain muffin
- trail mix of nuts and dried fruit
- pretzels
- crackers
- dry cereal
- single servings of whole-grain, low-sugar cereal, or
- yogurt [xi]

These foods digest slowly and release a steady supply of sugar, keeping the blood sugar level consistent throughout the day; no high- and low-sugar peaks to bring about a change in behavior. Feeding your child these foods at home will relieve the teacher of having to give your child a snack three times a day. Schools are for learning, teachers are for teaching, and home is where children should receive good nutrition to maintain their energy level.

Children who eat breakfast are two to five times more likely to consume at least two-thirds of the recommended amount of most vitamins and minerals, including iron. Eating breakfast has been shown to improve memory, grades, school attendance and punctuality in children. The USDA breakfast program in schools is in response to these findings[xii]

Finally, your child should drink plenty of water; at least eight glasses of water per day is recommended. The lack of sufficient water, a condition affecting the vast majority of Americans, also affects the brain. Because electrical impulses are impeded by even a slight dehydration of the brain, not getting enough water literally interferes with proper brain function.

A glass of water is eight fluid ounces of cool, pure water. That is in addition to whatever other fluids your child drinks. Soda, milk, orange juice and fruit-flavored drinks do not count and should be replaced with cool water. Tap water will do. If you want to do better, purchase a home filter so that the water tastes better.

Teaching your children how to have a healthy diet will have a bigger impact if you set the example. Eat right, get some exercise, and make a healthy lifestyle a family affair.

CHAPTER VII

SLEEP AND LEARNING

Scientists are still trying to learn exactly why people need sleep. Animal studies show that sleep is necessary for survival and sleep appears necessary for our nervous system to work properly. Additionally, because growth hormones are released during sleep, it is determined to be a dynamic time of healing and growth for children and young adults. It has also been determined that adequate sleep may help people maintain optimal emotional and social functioning while they are awake.

An important concern is what happens when we get too little sleep. It is known that too little sleep leaves us drowsy and unable to concentrate the next day. It also leads to impaired memory and physical performance and reduced ability to carry out math calculations. If sleep deprivation continues, hallucinations and mood swings may develop. Even if we feel that we have adapted to it, routine nightly sleep of fewer than six hours results in cognitive performance deficits. And if it is sustained night after night, lack of sleep can seriously impair the functioning of our central nervous system.

Sleep is no less important than food, drink or safety in the lives of children. Problems sleeping can cause symptoms such as fatigue, trouble concentrating, and inability to maintain attention, hyperactivity, headaches and anxiety. Many symptoms of sleep disorders are interpreted as ADHD and are discussed in Chapter XIII.

Given the serious side effects from a lack of sleep, the major findings in the 2004 Sleep in America Poll conducted by the National Sleep Foundation suggest that without immediate intervention, the incidence of sleep-related learning disabilities will increase into the twenty-second century, and the 2006 poll mirrors these findings.[xiii]

For example, sleep problems that affect more than one-third of elementary school-aged children include problems breathing during sleep, waking up during the night, difficulty falling asleep and daytime sleepiness. [xiv]

America's adolescents (5th-12th grade) are not getting the sleep they need either, and this lack of sleep gets worse as they progress through their teen years. The average fifth-grader sleeps an average of 8.4 hours on school nights, while a typical high school senior seeps just 6.9 hours. Over the course of a week, high school seniors miss nearly 12 hours of needed sleep!

More than half of adolescents say they know they get less sleep than they need to feel their best, while nine out of 10 parents believe their adolescent is getting enough sleep at least a few nights during the school week, leaving an "awareness gap" between parents and teens that suggests that parents are in the dark about their children's sleep.

The most impressive finding of the <u>Sleep in America Poll</u>[xv] is that parents do not identify their children's sleep problems as an issue that should be addressed. It is recommended that the bedroom be kept as a sleep haven, free from distractions, so that the system can begin to slow down and prepare for sleep. Instead, children are allowed to ignore the experts' advice to "wind down" with relaxing activities in the hour before bedtime.

In America, forty-three percent of school-aged children have a television in their bedroom, 30% of preschoolers, 18% of toddlers and 20% of infants also have a television in their bedroom.

Nearly all adolescents (97%) have at least one electronic item such as a TV, computer, phone or music device in their bedroom. On average, sixth-graders have more than two of these items in their bedroom, while twelfth-graders have about four. Seventy-six percent of adolescents report watching television as the most popular activity in the hour before bedtime, while other popular activities include surfing the Internet, instant-messaging and talking on the phone.

What Does this Mean for My Child?

In children, lack of sleep can be directly reflected in their behavior in a way that may not be immediately obvious. When adults are tired, they can either be grumpy or have low energy. But a child can become hyper, disagreeable; have extremes in behavior and exhibit difficulty learning.

Sleep deprivation can also lead to decreased attentiveness, decreased short-term memory, inconsistent performance and delayed response time. These can cause generally bad temper, problems in school, stimulant use and driving accidents (in fact, more than half of "asleep at the wheel" car accidents are caused by teens).

Ideally, a child should go to bed at the same time every night and wake up at the same time every morning, allowing for at least 8 or 9 hours of sleep. The amount of sleep a person needs increases if he or she has been deprived of sleep in previous days.

There is no magical number of hours of sleep required by all children in a certain age group. The amount of sleep each person needs depends on many factors, including age. Infants generally require about 16 hours a day, growing children need about 8 to 9.5 hours of sleep per night and as they progress through puberty, teens actually need more.

Independent investigators in Brazil, Japan and the United States have suggested that the internal biologic sleep-timing mechanism is reset along with the other changes in puberty. Teenagers are often incapable of falling asleep earlier. School schedules that force them out of bed at an early hour lead to a population of chronically sleep-deprived adolescents. The consideration given to starting high school an hour or two later would markedly improve the health and behavior of adolescents. Some cities have already implemented this change for the starting time of some high schools.

Snoring

Any child who snores may not be getting adequate sleep. A study of over 2,000 children who snored found significant cognitive differences between the children who snored and those who did not. Compared to non-snorers, children who snored showed significantly impaired attention, lower memory and IQ scores.[xvi] Children who snore are often nearly twice as likely as other children to have attention and hyperactivity problems, and the link is strong for other sleep problems.

Obstructive sleep apnea is a common medical condition that is now being identified in more and more children. During sleep the throat muscles relax, causing the snoring sound. In obstructive sleep apnea there is a cessation of breathing between snoring. This reduces the oxygen to the brain and disrupts the sleep cycle. This condition has been shown to cause heart disease, hypertension, depression, brain damage, etc. in adults. However, in children there is increasing evidence that Obstructive Sleep Apnea Syndrome can also have effects on respiration and physical growth and development.

Evidence indicates that in children with Sleep-Related Obstructive Breathing Disorder, neuro-cognitive deficits also occur. These include impairments in verbal and non-verbal intelligence, memory, psychomotor efficiency, sustained attention, concentration and psychosocial functioning. Symptoms of hyperactivity, impulsivity and distractibility, similar to ADHD, have also been reported. Not all kids with sleep apnea snore; however, even when they do, sleep apnea is often overlooked.

Poor sleep is a common feature of ADD—a problem that can be made worse by the use of stimulant medications such as Ritalin or Dexedrine. When parents of children with ADD are interviewed, they usually identify the children as poor or restless sleepers.[xvii] Sometimes it is obvious to parents that their children are not sleeping well, but the Sleep in America Poll suggests that most often, it is not.

Positive Benefits of Sleep

If for some reason your child is not getting enough sleep or has sleep problems, it should not be surprising that he also has behavioral and academic problems. By cutting down on sleep, we learn less, we develop less, we are less bright, we make worse decisions, we accomplish less, we are less productive, we are more prone to errors and we undermine our true intellectual potential!

However, just the opposite happens when we do get sufficient sleep. It has been known since the 1920s that sleep improves recall in learning and that a lack of sleep may cause a deficit in learning. However, only recently it has been demonstrated that sleep is *necessary* for learning! Without sleep we reduce the retention of facts we have learned the previous day.

It has been determined that when you learn a particular task, your performance is actually enhanced after a night of sleep. Without sleep, it appears that information learned is simply not retained. Information that is acquired while awake is actively altered, restructured, and strengthened during sleep. The brain becomes very active while new skills are being learned, but later during deep sleep the same part of the brain becomes active again. While deep sleep is important for some forms of learning, lighter stages of sleep appear to reinforce other kinds of learning.

The first five hours after learning seem crucial for memory to become consolidated. When learning motor-skill tasks, performance initially improves during training and continues to improve without further rehearsal across subsequent periods of sleep. Practicing a task makes you better at it, but deep sleep within five hours after practice makes you better still.

What to Do

A factor to take into consideration is that sleep deprivation is cumulative. Children who are not getting enough sleep will incur an increasing "sleep debt" over time, causing them to perform less well and feel more sleepy with each succeeding day of insufficient sleep. Parents should look for some of the following signs that their child's sleep may be insufficient either in quantity or quality:

- Your child does not wake up readily in the morning, but must be awakened, sometimes with great difficulty.
- Your child often has a rushed or missed breakfast in the morning because he or she frequently oversleeps.
- Your child appears sleepy during the day either to the teacher, to you or to both. Some sleep-deprived children fall asleep in school, particularly when they are bored
- You or the teacher notes that your child is having trouble concentrating on work or finishing tasks.
- Your child seems irritable, particularly late in the day. This may also be reflected in behavior problems and unexpectedly poor academic performance.
- Your child falls asleep after coming home from school in the afternoon.
- Your child sleeps much longer and later on weekends than during the week (repaying an accumulated 'sleep debt").

You can better define whether your child is getting adequate sleep by keeping a sleep diary for one or two weeks, noting the times your child goes to bed and awakens, and whether waking is spontaneous. The diary should also record observations of daytime sleepiness, irritability, ability to concentrate and performance of schoolwork.

In addition watching your child sleep at random times through the night may also be revealing. Record these observations in the sleep diary as well. Restless and fitful sleep may suggest poor sleep quality. This can sometimes be caused by upper airway problems that may need the attention of the pediatrician. In the extreme, some of these children will exhibit sleep apnea, usually accompanied by loud snoring and chest movements that are irregular and labored.

If this is the case, contact your pediatrician immediately and inquire about a sleep study to determine exactly what is going on and how best to treat your child.

In other instances, restless sleep may be the result of medications that the child is taking. In any event, the sleep diary should be shared with your child's pediatrician, who may be helpful if you are seeing daytime symptoms of sleepiness, poor performance or deteriorating behavior that you suspect may be due to a sleep problem.

Sleep serves a variety of physiological functions, one of which is the generation of energy reserves needed for academic achievement. If we can accept this as true, it would appear that any child would benefit greatly from the energy generated by additional amounts of sleep. This is especially true if the child has been diagnosed with learning disabilities.

For some learning-disabled children, the school day is far too long. These children have the stamina to stay attentive for about four hours, which gets them through the morning until lunch. The afternoon for them is a haze of tasks which they struggle to achieve.

With this challenge and constant stress upon their nervous system, it would follow that some children would benefit from a nap right after school for three reasons:

·   it relaxes an exhausted nervous system,

·   solidifies the learning that has taken place during the school day, and

·   generates the energy reserves needed for the challenges of doing homework, which should be done only after the child has had a nap or other rest period.

If your child is having academic and behavioral problems, one of the things to do is to see that he is sleeping well. Be sure to request an exploration of his sleep patterns in the school evaluation, and then, if he snores, have your pediatrician or family doctor explore the extent of the problem and request a referral to a respiratory therapist, the professional who specializes in solutions to this problem.

Although there is not one sure way to raise a good sleeper, it is encouraging to know that most children have the ability to sleep well. The key is to try, from early on, to establish healthy sleep habits that may last a lifetime.

To prioritize sleep for all family members, including adolescents, the National Sleep Foundation offers these tips:

·   Set a regular bedtime and wake-up schedule (even on the weekends) so that an adolescent can achieve nine or more hours of sleep every night.

·   Encourage a relaxing bedtime routine such as reading for fun or taking a warm bath or shower.

·   Keep the bedroom comfortable—dark, cool and quiet.

·   Remove TVs, computers and other distractions from the bedroom and set limits on usage before bedtime.

·   Avoid all caffeine after lunchtime.

For many kids bedtime is no fun, and for many parents getting younger children to go to bed and stay there can be frustrating. Here are some hints to help with the task.[xviii]

·   Get involved and make going to bed a pleasant experience.

·   Start the process at the same time each night; this helps the body to get into a routine.

·   Set a quiet time approximately 30 minutes before bedtime: no computer, television, stimulating music, video games or surfing the Net to allow the system to begin to slow down.

·   Follow a bedtime routine that is calming, such as taking a warm bath or reading.

·   Quiet, slow-paced, simplistic music can also help your child to fall asleep. Music products are available that are designed to help fulfill this function.

·   Avoid using the bed for activities other than sleep in order to maintain an association between getting into bed and sleeping.

·   Don't have a TV in your child's room. As we have discovered, kids with a TV in their room sleep less. If there is a TV, turn it off when it's time to sleep.

·   See that teeth are brushed, the child is tucked in and the lights are off.

When Your Child Won't Stay in Bed[xxvii]

·   Return your child to bed right away; no arguing or bargaining.

·   If you child cries or protests, wait a few minutes, then go back to check on him or her.

·   If the child continues to cry or call for you, wait a little longer each time before you go to check.

·   Remind your child that it is time to go to sleep, and if he/she stays quiet, you will come back to check on him or her in a few minutes.

While not all sleep problems can be solved with environmental and schedule alterations, there is good evidence that a significant percentage of sleep problems can benefit significantly from such changes. Research is now shedding light of how such changes can also help children and adolescents with "behavior problems" or "psychological problems."

It is important to note that this absolutely does not mean that if your son or daughter was diagnosed with ADHD or with any other diagnosis, the diagnosis was made in error. It does mean, however, that if you give your pediatrician or other health professional information about your child's sleep, it might produce a different kind of diagnosis, and therefore a different kind of treatment recommendation. Even if the original diagnosis proves accurate, a good sleep hygiene routine can often improve the performance of your child beyond any improvements seen from other things you may be trying.

CHAPTER VIII

TOXIC METALS

Author's Note: While preparing the first draft of this manuscript, the author experienced a sudden worsening of blurred vision, difficulty with cognitive processing, loss of memory and other symptoms, which necessitated a delay in completing the first draft of the manuscript.

Immediate evaluation by the medical community revealed that general practice physicians do not have medical training in heavy metal toxicity and could not diagnose the condition. This was true at a major hospital on the west coast and at the primary care facility of a major Midwestern university. Two physicians informed that they were unable to assist me with my condition or that of an older brother who was suffering similar symptoms and had been diagnosed with Alzheimer's disease. It seems that metal toxicity is a medical specialty known as forensics and general practitioners do not receive this training.

A licensed chiropractor practicing kinesiology diagnosed mercury toxicity from amalgam fillings. Chelation therapies initiated at home resulted in improved symptoms in three days, thereby verifying the diagnosis, and after a six-month period the writer is almost symptom-free.

This experience, along with much research and resulting insight into a lifetime of problems with memory and learning, led not only to the inclusion of this chapter in the manuscript, but renewed determination to complete the project.

Heavy Metals

About 40 electropositive elements are natural constituents of the earth's crust, and having a density greater than five, they are commonly referred to as "heavy" metals. These metals differ widely in their chemical properties and degree of toxicity. Of this group, mercury, lead, aluminum and cadmium are invariably toxic and a source of concern in the environment.

Toxic means that they cause biological changes in the body resulting in severe illnesses and other disabilities. Mercury in dental fillings and other dental appliances is probably the single greatest source of mercury toxicity in people today. Others include eating fish and receiving vaccines with thimerosal. Some physicians suggest that amalgam fillings and immunizations could be part of the explanation for the explosion of learning problems and autism in children since World War II, a time period corresponding with the introduction and widespread use of mercury amalgams.

Dental Amalgams

According to the American Dental Association (ADA), "Dental amalgam is considered a safe, affordable and durable material that has been used to restore the teeth of more than 100 million Americans. It contains a mixture of metals such as silver, copper and tin, in addition to mercury, which chemically binds these components into a hard, stable and safe substance. Dental amalgam has been studied and reviewed extensively, and has established a record of safety and effectiveness."

Ponder that along with the fact that in 1988 the Environmental Protection Agency (EPA) declared scrap dental amalgam a hazardous waste and in 1989 this same agency declared that amalgams are a hazardous substance. Interestingly, the metallic mercury used by dentists to manufacture dental amalgam is shipped to dental offices as a hazardous material. Outside your mouth it has to be stored in unbreakable, tightly sealed containers away from heat, is not to be touched and has to be stored under liquid glycerin or photographic fixer solution.

When it is placed in the teeth it is labeled "nontoxic." But when it is taken out of the teeth it is labeled "toxic." As an unidentified member of the International Academy of Oral Medicine and Toxicology states it: "I am just not comfortable somehow with a material (mercury fillings) that I cannot legally throw in the trash, bury in the ground, send to a landfill for disposal, (or legally handle with my bare hands), but which, they say, I can safely put in your mouth...."xx[xix]i

In the mouth, highly toxic methyl mercury vapors from amalgams are released continually. Simple activities such as chewing gum, drinking hot liquids and brushing teeth can increase the release of methyl mercury even more. Yet, the ADA does not advise removing existing amalgam fillings from teeth.

And, if you are a thinking person and decide to have your amalgams removed and replaced with a non-toxic material, we are warned that the most important thing is to find a dentist who can remove your amalgams safely. Any dentist can technically replace your amalgams, but if they don't employ proper precautions, much of the methyl mercury in your fillings will go straight to your brain, where as a neurotoxin it impedes neural function and can interfere with learning.

Thimerosal is the other common source of mercury poisoning. It is a mercury-based preservative widely used in vaccines, including those routinely administered to children. Thimerosal contains close to 50 percent ethyl mercury by weight. Children are particularly sensitive to the mercury, as their nervous systems are still rapidly developing. Years ago, health-related organizations such as the American Academy of Pediatrics (AAP) and the Centers for Disease Control and Prevention recommended that thimerosal be removed from vaccines as soon as possible, yet it's still present in many vaccinations including diphtheria, pertussis and tetanus (DPT) which are required before a child can enter school.

Recently a congressional hearing was convened on the adverse effects of mercury in the body, especially in children, and its relationship to autism. The hearings concluded a potential connection between autism and mercury toxicity and recommended the discontinued use of thimerosal in vaccines.[xxix]

As a result of recent legislation, many vaccine producers have begun to voluntarily lower (not remove) the amount of thimerosal used in the vaccines they produce, flu vaccine being the one exception.[xx]xx

Lead is usually absorbed into the body by drinking contaminated water from lead pipes or by eating lead-based paint in older houses. Fumes from lead-based paints, automobile exhaust and polluted air from industrial plants or cigarette smoke may all contain lead. Lead has been recognized as a danger to children and adults for some time, and while some of these sources, such as lead-based paint and leaded gasoline, have been discontinued over the past few decades, their effects still show up in the environment.

According to the National Health and Nutrition Examination

Survey, the prevalence of lead toxicity in U.S. children ranged from 1.5 percent for upper-income children living in recently built houses in the suburbs, to 36.7 percent for children residing in older homes in large cities. Children are more susceptible to lead absorption than adults, whose lead toxicity is generally related to occupational exposure.

Aluminum is a heavy metal found everywhere and, therefore, is the toxic metal most commonly found in toxic individuals. Antiperspirants, toothpaste, dental amalgams, baby power, cosmetics and cigarette filters and smoke all contain aluminum. We ingest it in some drinking water, some commercial teas, cheese, white flour, baking powder, aspirin, antacids and table salt. We cook with it too; some pots and pans contain aluminum and the aluminum in the metal cookware leaches out into the food cooked in it, particularly acidic foods like tomatoes. Aluminum may also leach out of aluminum foil or cans into food and beverages.

According to a report in The Lancet in 1989, many infant formulas contain aluminum. This report revealed that human breast milk contained 5-20 micrograms per liter of aluminum, cow's milk-based formulas contained 20 times the amount of aluminum in human breast milk, and soy-based formulas contained 100 times as much.

Cadmium is also very toxic. Tobacco smoke from cigarette, cigar, or pipe contains cadmium; studies have shown that cigarette smokers have higher levels of cadmium in their body than nonsmokers. You can also accumulate cadmium from second-hand smoke. This fact has led some courts to show deference to non-smoking parents during custody cases. In addition to tobacco smoke and plastics, common sources of cadmium exposure include drinking water, fertilizer, fungicides, pesticides, soil, air pollution, refined grains, rice, coffee, tea and soft drinks.

The health effects in children are expected to be similar to those in adults (kidney, lung and intestinal damage). We don't know if cadmium causes birth defects in people because cadmium does not readily go from a pregnant woman's body into the developing child, but some portion can cross the placenta and it can be found in breast milk. The babies of animals exposed to high levels of cadmium during pregnancy had changes in behavior and learning ability. Cadmium may also affect birth weight and the skeleton in developing animals.

Animal studies also indicate that more cadmium is absorbed into the body if the diet is low in calcium, protein or iron or is high in fat. A few studies show that younger animals absorb more cadmium and are more likely to lose bone and bone strength than adults.

Like other metals, cadmium stays in the body for a long time and accumulates after long-term exposure to even low levels. Fish, plants, and animals accumulate cadmium from the environment and as a consequence there are low levels of the metal in most all foods, with the highest levels found in shellfish, liver and kidney meats.[xxx]

What Does This Mean for My Child

In children, symptoms of mercury toxicity include learning disorders and memory loss, irritability, fatigue, vision problems, attention deficit disorders, hyperactivity, poor visual-motor coordination and a host of other conditions that are labeled as learning disabilities. As toxic metal accumulates in the body, these problems become worse over time as the metals interact with other nutrients, making some minerals perform more than normal and others not perform vital functions at all.

Over the past decade, the prevalence of autism and other neuro-developmental disorders such as attention deficit disorder have been increasing at epidemic proportions and many experts believe that mercury from vaccines is at least partly to blame.

Aluminum has been implicated for years in several brain diseases. Hyperactivity, memory disturbances and learning disabilities may result from even mildly elevated levels of aluminum. Inhibition of communication between nerve cells and impaired motor coordination may also result.

Lead toxicity in children can delay growth, impair motor skill development and affect the way nerves communicate with each other; it also interferes with the brain's ability to utilize dopamine and serotonin, which control behavior and emotions. Toxicity from this metal can also cause attention deficits, behavioral disorders, lower I.Q., poor eye-hand coordination and low vocabulary and reading skills.

Additional Concerns

It is evident that politics and government are not going to have a significant environmental impact in the near future and even if legislation were enacted immediately, it would take 50 years to clean up the environmental damage done since World War II.

However, all is not lost. On a more positive note, as for amalgams and the American Dental Association, it takes only a moment to consider the consequences to our economic system if they did publicly acknowledge that amalgams are toxic and that dentists have placed one of the most toxic non-radioactive substances known to man in the mouths of about 100,000 million Americans since World War II.

Such an admission would result in lawsuits against dentists, dentists would have to be retrained, most would not be able to practice again, insurance companies would go out of business and all this would have a significant impact upon the economy, causing untold economic disaster throughout the country.

A thinking person quickly realizes that the ADA, being composed of rational beings, is more than aware of the consequences of putting a toxic element into the mouths of people and it is probably wondering how this happened in the first place. Its position on the use of amalgam fillings, it seems, is simply a ploy to head off economic disaster for the dental profession as well as for the country at large.

A thinking person will also be grateful for this ploy by the ADA, then read the research and on his/her own take appropriate action.

There is a simple method of addressing heavy metal toxicity, and the first step is for determined parents to accept that their attention would best be focused on protecting their child rather than getting involved in politics and lawsuits. The recommended methods do not include doctors and drug companies and prescriptions for drugs as toxic as any heavy metal. So let's leave the environment to the environmentalists, the politics to the politicians, and focus our efforts on parenting.

What to Do

If your child has dental amalgams, the best course of action is to consult a competent dentist who can safely remove them. And if you smoke, for your child's sake, you might consider quitting and making your home smoke-free. Also, you might begin to read product labels and begin avoiding those with high aluminum content. Stainless steel cookware is another way to avoid aluminum. Waxed paper to cover food is not as convenient, but it has not been identified as containing toxic ingredients as have plastic and aluminum foil.

The best approach is complete avoidance of mercury in any form, or at least a significant reduction in the amount consumed. As an alternative to fish, most sardines have little-to-no mercury since they are so small and you can also take a high-quality purified <u>fish oil or cod liver oil</u> to safely receive the health benefits of fish without the mercury.

Since some manufacturers have developed thimerosal-free vaccines it is possible to get childhood vaccines without thimerosal. However; you will have to ask your doctor to check the package insert and provide a written guarantee that the vaccine is mercury-free. Even then you will not know for sure, as the package inserts, which are supposed to detail exactly what is in a vaccine, <u>may not be accurate</u>.

Removing Heavy Metal

Today chelation therapy (pronounced key-LAY-shun) is thought to be a safe and effective way to rid your body and your child's body of heavy metal. When chelating agents are used to eliminate toxic metals such as lead from the body, essential nutrients are better able to do their job.

There are many foods that will chelate toxins; chlorella (a sea weed) and cilantro (Chinese parsley or coriander) are the simplest methods of all. Both provide advantages, including an outstanding ability to eliminate toxins, pesticides and heavy metals from the body. Removing toxic metals from your child's body is as simple as adding new ingredients to the diet.

If you need help, food pharmacies (health food stores) usually employ trained nutritional counselors. Just tell them what you are trying to do and they will assist you in finding what you need. Here is one of the better references you will find at your health food store; this author has used it for years. Here are some excerpts:[xxxii]

·   Cilantro removes unwanted mercury. Add to your soups and salads, or use like lettuce on sandwiches.

·   Calcium prevents lead from depositing in the body. Use the chelated form with magnesium only; other forms contain lead. 2,000 mg per day is recommended. Follow the directions on the bottle or eat foods high in calcium.

·   Kelp (sea weed), chlorella, cilantro, and/or alfalfa contain essential minerals, especially calcium and magnesium. They also remove unwanted metal deposits. Add them to soups, salads, casseroles, sprinkle on scrambled eggs, add to omelets; be creative.

·   Vitamin C plus bioflavonoids with rutin neutralizes the effect of lead (the bioflavonoids and rutin are important). 2,000 to 10,000 mg per day, depending upon whether you are preventing or chelating.

·   Kyolic garlic capsules help to bind and excrete lead.

When heavy metals are chelated, vitamin B-12 is usually leached from the system also. B-12 is necessary for nervous system function, so be sure to supplement the B-12 so that the body's store does not become depleted.

Here is a simple formula to prevent further build-up of toxins in the system. All ingredients are available at your local food pharmacy or health food store.

Cilantro Chelation Pesto

4 cloves garlic

1/3 cup Brazil nuts (selenium)

1/3 cup sunflower seeds (cysteine)

1/3 cup pumpkin seeds (zinc, magnesium)

2 cups packed fresh cilantro (coriander, Chinese parsley, vitamin A)

4 tablespoons lemon juice (vitamin C)

1/3 cup flaxseed oil

2 tsp dulse powder, Sea salt to taste

Process the cilantro and flaxseed oil in a blender until the coriander (cilantro) is chopped. Add the garlic, nuts and seeds, dulse and lemon juice and mix until the mixture is finely blended into a paste. Add a pinch of sea salt to taste and blend again. If available, store in dark glass jars. It freezes well, so purchase cilantro in season and fill enough jars to last through the year.[xxxiii]

Two teaspoons of the pesto every day for two weeks reportedly will accomplish the objective of clearing heavy metals from the body. Just repeat the two-week treatment every 6 to 12 months for prevention. It tastes good too; this author extended her treatment past the two-week period. It makes an excellent snack food. Spread it on pasta, English muffins, scrambled eggs, or crackers with tea.

And remember, giving your child Ritalin will take less time and effort, but this recipe is good for the whole family. It tastes good, and it will not stunt your child's growth or cause permanent damage to his nervous system.

STOP

Before proceeding with Part II of this book, if there is anything that you did not understand in Part I go back and reread the section for clarification.

A Summary of Important Information from Part I

- The incidence of learning disabilities in the average school population is increasing at a rate of 10% to 20% every 10 years.
- This increase is attributed to environmental trauma, which impacts the central nervous system of the developing child.
- Learning disabilities may result from physical, emotional or psychological trauma to the brain or other parts of the central nervous system.
- Without sufficient exercise, the physical body does not develop and higher cognitive functions do not integrate.
- The way in which parents interact socially with their child will impact the child's ability to learn.

·   By eating a poor diet, children are doomed to a future of mediocre intelligence, poor eyesight, decreased hearing and delayed and deficient verbal skills.

·   Lack of sleep may cause a deficit in learning. Adequate sleep improves recall in learning and recently it has been demonstrated that sleep is necessary for learning!

·   In the body, toxins from heavy metals produce disorders which are labeled as learning disabilities. Fortunately, removing toxic metals from your or your child's body is a simple, uncomplicated process that can be done at home.

·   Parents can take specific actions to remove, reduce or remedy the impact of any of the identified environmental influences in their child's environment.

·   The good news from recent research suggests that new learning experiences can alter the damaged neural connections in the brain. It is never too late to create positive change in a child's life.

Introduction to Part II

Part II is designed to assist you in working knowledgably with the schools in determining whether special education is appropriate for your child. It is the next step toward being sure that the school is providing the kind of classroom support that is needed to support all the hard work that you have done, are doing or are going to do at home.

Part II is organized to assist you with making the decision to place or not place your child in special education. It begins with a summary of the laws governing special education and your rights under the law and outlines your role and function as parent advocate for an appropriate education for your child.

CHAPTER IX

LAWS THAT GOVERN SPECIAL EDUCATION

There are four major federal laws that govern and guarantee your child's rights as a participant in public education.

The Individuals with Disabilities Education Act (IDEA) of 1997 is a federal law that governs all special education services for children in the United States. Under IDEA, in order for a child to be eligible for special education he must be in one of the following categories: serious emotional disturbance, learning disabilities, mental retardation, traumatic brain injury, autism, vision and hearing impairments, physical disabilities and other health impairments.

The Individuals with Disabilities Education Improvement Act of 2004 (IDEA) calls for increased accountability for states, school districts, and schools; greater choices for parents and students, particularly those attending low-performing schools; more flexibility for states and local educational agencies in the use of federal education dollars; and a stronger emphasis on reading, especially for our youngest children.

Section 504 of the Rehabilitation Act of 1973 is a civil rights statute that requires that schools not discriminate against children with disabilities and provide them with reasonable accommodations. It covers all programs or activities, whether public or private, that receive federal financial assistance.

Reasonable accommodations include un-timed tests, sitting in front of the class, modified homework and the provision of necessary services. Typically, children covered under Section 504 either have less severe disabilities than those covered under IDEA or have disabilities that do not fit within the eligibility categories of IDEA. Under Section 504, any person who has an impairment that substantially limits a major life activity is considered disabled. Learning and social development are included under the list of major life activities.

The Americans with Disabilities Act (ADA) requires all educational institutions other than those operated by religious organizations to meet the needs of children with psychiatric problems. The ADA prohibits the denial of educational services, programs or activities to students with disabilities and prohibits discrimination against all such students.

Elementary and Secondary Education Act (The No Child Left Behind Act of 2001) ensures that all children have a fair, equal and significant opportunity to obtain a high-quality education and reach, at a minimum, proficiency on challenging state academic achievement standards and state academic assessments.

Parent Rights in the Special Education Process

Your rights are numerous and far supersede those of the school district. The law is designed to provide the best for your child and to provide guidelines for school districts to ensure that your child receives those services guaranteed by the law. The government's objective is to ensure that every citizen has an equal opportunity for success as a contributing member of the society. Here are your rights, simplified for immediate review.

· Your child is entitled to a free, appropriate public education that meets the unique educational needs of your child, at no cost to you as parents.

· You will be notified whenever the school wishes to evaluate your child for potential special education needs, wants to change your child's educational placement or refuses your request for an evaluation or a change in placement.

· You may request an evaluation if you think your child needs special education or related services or if you don't agree that it is appropriate.

· Initially, meet with your child's teacher to share your   concerns and request an evaluation by the school's child study team. (Make all requests for evaluations and services dated and in writing. Always be careful to keep a copy of everything for your records, including observations reported by your child's teachers and any communications between home and school, such as notes, reports, letters, etc. and document phone calls. An attorney will request these.)

· Parents can also request independent professional evaluations.

· You should be asked by your school to provide "informed consent" (meaning you understand and agree in writing to the evaluation and educational program decisions for your child). Your consent is voluntary and you can always change your mind.

·   You may obtain an independent evaluation if you disagree with the outcome of the school's evaluation.

·   The findings of the school's evaluation team are not final. You have the right to appeal their conclusions and determination. The school is required to provide you with information about how to make an appeal.

·   You may request re-evaluation if you think your child's current educational placement is no longer appropriate. The school must re-evaluate your child at least every three years, but your child's educational program must be reviewed at least once during each calendar year.

·   You may have your child tested for special education needs in the language he or she knows best.

·   You may review all of your child's records and obtain copies of these records, but the school may charge you a reasonable fee for making copies.

·   Only you as parents and those persons directly involved in the education of your child may have access to personal records. If you feel that any of the information in your child's records is inaccurate, misleading or violates the privacy or other rights of your child, you may request that the information be changed. If the school refuses your request, you have the right to request a hearing to challenge the questionable information in your child's records; you may also file a complaint with your state education agency.

·   You must be fully informed by the school about all of the rights provided to you and your child under the law.

·   You may participate in the development of your child's Individualized Education Program (IEP) or, in the case of a child younger than four years old, the development of an Individualized Family Service Plan (IFSP). The IEP and the IFSP are written statements of the educational program designed to meet your child's unique needs. The school must make every possible effort to notify you of the IEP or IFSP meeting and to arrange the meeting at a time and place that is convenient for both you and the school.

·   Examples of categories of services in IEPs include: Occupational Therapy, Physical Therapy, Speech and Language Therapy and/or the provision of a classroom aide.

·   You may participate in all IEP or IFSP team decisions, including placement.

·   You may request an IEP or IFSP meeting at any time during the school year.

·   You may have your child educated in the least restrictive school setting possible. The school should make every effort to develop an educational program that will provide your child with the services and supports needed so that he can be taught with children who do not have disabilities.

·   You may request a due process hearing or voluntary mediation to resolve differences with the school that can't be resolved informally. Make your request in writing, date your request and keep a copy for your records.

·   You should be kept informed about your child's progress at least as often as parents of children who do not have disabilities.

Advocate for your Child

Children with special needs are guaranteed rights to services in school under federal and state laws. The process, however, can be confusing and intimidating. Here are some tips:

·   Parents must be proactive and take necessary steps to make sure their child receives appropriate services. There have been many advances in the assessment of learning abilities. If your school district is still using the old Wechsler Intelligence Scale for Children (WISC) you have the right to insist that your child be assessed with an instrument such as the Cognitive Assessment System, which measures processing weaknesses rather than general intelligence. There is a need to know specifics about your child's disability and this test will find them.

·   You should demand to know exactly how the disability is exhibited in the classroom in terms of specific behaviors, learning strengths and weaknesses, what interventions are available and how identified weaknesses will be accommodated. The law insures your right to know!

·   Parents should request copies of their school district's Section 504 plan. This is especially important when a school district refuses services. This plan states how learning problems will be accommodated when the student does not meet eligibility for special education.

·   If the school district does not respond to your request, you can contact a U.S. Department of Education Office or Civil Rights Regional Office for assistance. If the school district refuses services under the IDEA or Section 504 or both, you may choose to challenge this decision through a due process hearing.

· It may also be necessary to retain your own attorney if you decide to appeal a school's decision.

CHAPTER X

THE INDIVIDUALIZED EDUCATION PLAN

The Individualized Education Plan (IEP) is a written document that outlines the child's special education plan by defining goals for the school year, services needed to help the child meet those goals, and a method of evaluating the student's progress. When all parties have agreed upon goals, objectives and services by affixing their signature to the document, the IEP becomes the legal document stating how the child will be educated.

Planning the IEP creates an opportunity for teachers, parents, school administrators, related services personnel and students (when age-appropriate) to work together to improve educational results for children with disabilities. The IEP is the cornerstone of a quality education for each child.

It is in this meeting that decisions are made that will determine how he is instructed, what support services he will need, as well as, the environment in which he will receive them. It is in this meeting that you, the parent, can have the greatest impact upon the future of your child's education and it is at this point in the process that the parent can be most effective as an advocate.

The IEP Meeting

Following assessment, the local education agency officials and others involved in the child's educational program meet to discuss education-related goals and develop the IEP. By law, the following people must be invited to attend the IEP meeting: [xxxiv]

· One or both of the child's parents

- The child's teacher or prospective teacher
- A representative of the public agency (local education agency, or school district) who is qualified to provide or supervise the provision of special education (other than the child's teacher)
- The child, if appropriate
- Other individuals, at the discretion of the parent or agency (such as a physician, advocate or neighbor).

Rules for Conducting the IEP Meeting

With the 1997 Reauthorization of IDEA (P.L. 105-17)

- Parents now must be included as "members of any group that makes decisions on the educational placement of the child."
- IEP meetings must be held at least annually, but may be held more often if needed.
- Parents may request a review or revision of the IEP at any time.
- While teachers and school personnel may come prepared for the meeting with an outline of goals and objectives, the IEP is not complete until it has been thoroughly discussed and all parties agree to the written document.
- Parents are entitled to participate in the IEP meeting as equal participants with suggestions and opinions regarding their child's education. They, too, may bring a list of suggested goals and objectives, as well as additional information that may be pertinent, to the IEP meeting.
- The local education agency (LEA) must attempt to schedule the IEP meeting at a time and place agreeable to both school staff and parents.
- School districts must notify parents in a timely manner so that they will have an opportunity to attend.
- The notification must indicate the purpose of the meeting (i.e. to discuss transition services, behavior problems interfering with learning, academic growth).

Parents may encounter stipulations presented by school personnel such as a predetermined number of pages, or only a certain number of goals and objectives are allowed on the IEP, or the objective has to fit in the field length on their computer program. There is nothing in the federal law that supports these types of statements or stipulations

While parents should not accept misinformation concerning the IEP, it is in everyone's best interest to remember that both parents and teachers share a common goal: to develop a program that will be appropriate for the child with learning disability. By sharing information and knowledge, parents and schools can collaborate to develop a truly effective IEP. If for some reason you do not agree with the proposed IEP, or your ideas, goals or objectives have not been considered and included, your recourse is to not sign the document.

Following is a summary of what must be contained in the IEP:

·	The student's disability

·	A vision statement of the student's long-term goal (one to five years in future).

·	Description of how the student's disability affects his progress in the classroom.

·	Short-term goals, based upon the child's learning strengths and weaknesses,

·	How the child's progress toward these goals will be measured and how the goals will be evaluated

·	Accommodations and modifications to be used in the classroom

·	For a student with behavior or emotional issues that interferes with his learning, the IEP should contain a program designed to teach the student appropriate behavior and social skills as well as all behavioral management techniques to be used.

·	Summer services

·	Transportation needs

·	Type of placement.

Content of an IEP must Include the Following

·	A statement of the child's present level of educational performance. This should include both academic and non-academic aspects of his/her performance.

·	A statement of annual goals that the student may reasonably accomplish in the next 12 months. This statement should also include a series of measurable, intermediate objectives for each goal. This will help both the parents and educators know whether the child is progressing and benefiting from his/her education. The development of specific, well-defined goals and objectives is crucial to your child receiving an appropriate education.

·   Appropriate objective criteria, evaluation procedures and schedules for determining, at least annually, whether the child is achieving the short-term objectives set out in the IEP. (For example, "How are we judging whether intervention is successful?" "How long will my child be in this program?")

·   A description of all specific special education and related services, including individualized instruction and related supports and services, to be provided (e.g. occupational therapy, physical therapy, speech therapy, transportation, recreation). This includes the extent to which the child will participate in regular educational programs.

·   The initiation date and duration of each of the services, as determined above, to be provided (this can include extended school year services). You may include the person who will be responsible for implementing each service.

·   If your child is 16 years old or older, the IEP must include a description of transitional services (coordinated set of activities designed to assist the student in movement from school to post-school activities).

Related Services in the IEP

Students with disabilities have a right to related services to help them learn and receive the maximum benefit from their educational programs. Related services, according to IDEA, consist of "transportation and such developmental, corrective and other supportive services as are required to assist a child with a disability to benefit from special education." These services are to be determined on an individualized basis, not by the disability or category of the disability.

If a child needs any of these "related services" to benefit from his/her education, they must be written into the IEP. Frequency and duration of services, as well as relevant objectives, should be included. Related services as defined by IDEA may include, but are not limited to the following:

- audiological (hearing) evaluation and services
- counseling services
- early identification and assessment of disabilities in children
- medical services (for diagnostic or evaluation purposes only)
- occupational therapy
- parent counseling and training
- physical therapy
- psychological services
- recreation
- rehabilitation counseling
- school health services
- social work services
- speech pathology
- transportation

The regulation does not limit related services to those specifically mentioned above. If a child requires a particular service to benefit from special education and that service is developmental, corrective or supportive, it is also a "related" service and should be provided. It does not have to be expressly listed in the regulations. Examples of these kinds of services may include a full- or part-time aide or assistive technology such as a computer.

IEP Goals, Objectives, Evaluation

An IEP should include goals and objectives specific to each child's unique needs. Goals may be broad, such as "This student will learn basic information not learned in earlier grades due to developmental immaturity," or "John will learn basic developmental math and reading skills not learned in earlier grades because of developmental immaturity" or more specifically, "John will recognize, write and know the place value of all numbers 1-100." Educational objectives are tailored to a child's individual needs and based on the long-term goal. They describe the process by which the child may reach the goal and how a child's progress will be monitored.

For example:

Goal: During the course of the year, John will learn basic developmental math and reading skills not learned in earlier grades.

Objective I: In a one-on-one situation in the resource room, John will learn basic developmental math and reading from the Resource Specialist. The sessions will occur at least four times a week, and last at least 30 minutes.

Objective II: After receiving both verbal and visual cues, John will demonstrate his knowledge by writing, reciting and recognizing all letters and numerals in print with 90 percent accuracy.

Objective III: When given visual and verbal clues, John will demonstrate knowledge of the phonemic sounds of letters and quantities represented by numerals.

Objective IV: The resource specialist will document careful observations and send weekly reports to John's parents as well as to his homeroom teacher. This support will begin September 1 and continue until December 15, excluding pre-determined school holidays.

The above objectives specifically state:

- the service to be provided (development of basic math and reading skills),

- the professional who will be providing that service (the resource specialist),

- the setting in which the service will be provided (resource room),

- how often the service will be provided (four times a week), and

- the length of the service (30 minutes per session from September 1 through December 15).

The evaluation component of the objective addresses the question "How will we know whether John is making progress?" In this case, the resource specialist will determine whether John is meeting the goal of 90 percent accuracy in writing and recognizing letters and numerals and send reports to his homeroom teacher and family each week. Other evaluation methods may include test-taking, videotaping, peer reports, daily logs, checklists, computer printouts and worksheets. Goals can have more than one objective. The above information is only one example of an objective to meet the goal of developing basic skills.

What If You and the School Don't Agree?

Within the law, there are specific procedural safeguards to protect your child's rights. If you and the school disagree on the placement, educational program or other matters surrounding your child's education, you may want to utilize one or more of the following approaches:

· Discussion or conference with school staff. Staff may include the teachers, counselors or principal.

· An IEP review. You may request an IEP review at any time.

· Negotiation or mediation. Mediation is a voluntary process as described in IDEA in which a neutral third person (mediator) assists parties (parents and the school) to work together to resolve their dispute. All states must have a mediation process established that meets the requirements of IDEA, including maintaining a list of qualified mediators and bearing the cost of the mediation process.

Neither party may be required to use mediation. The mediator cannot force either party to accept a resolution to the dispute. If a mutually satisfactory agreement is reached on some or all of the issues, a written agreement is set forth. Discussions that occur in mediation are confidential and may not be used as evidence in subsequent proceedings. Mediation must be available as a dispute resolution option, but may not be used to deny or delay the parental right to a due process hearing.

You may request a due process hearing if you do not agree with your child's identification, evaluation or educational placement. This is a legal proceeding and you should obtain legal advice.

Any individual or organization may file a complaint alleging that the local educational agency has violated a requirement of IDEA. The complaint must be written and signed; it must cite the specific IDEA requirement that was violated and the facts upon which the allegation is made.

The state educational agency must resolve the issues of the complaint within 60 calendar days after it is filed.

Many parents seek assistance from education advocates or disability advocates. Each state has a federally funded Parent Training Information Center (PTI) that provides information and assistance to parents facing the educational process.

After The IEP Is Completed

Once the IEP is completed, ongoing communication between school and parents is essential to a child's success. The family and the school need to work together for the child to receive maximum benefit. The IEP is a working document that can change. It should represent a program flexible enough to respond to the changing needs and skills of the person with learning disability. The IEP team can meet to discuss changes or additions to a child's plan at any time. The child's parents or school representatives may request a meeting when either party feels the IEP needs to be adjusted to a child's current needs.

CHAPTER XI

EDUCATIONAL ADVOCACY

Before beginning advocacy for your child's education, it would be helpful to be sure that you have addressed any trauma, injuries, nutritional or health problems and have had his vision and hearing checked so that you are assured that you are doing or have done your part at home to prepare your child for learning. The goal is to insure that what you are going to ask the schools to do is a complement to all the work that has been done at home and not a substitute for any work that should have been done.

If you have been informed that your child is not achieving as well as might be expected for his grade level, initially it might be a good idea to welcome the exploration of your child's learning problem at the student team meeting and identify why he is not learning. You may gain information that gives you a better idea of how to help him at home. At least it gives you an opportunity to talk with all the players all at once, get their input and do some problem-solving before making a decision about special education. This process will provide all the information needed to give "informed consent" for modification of the educational program.

Why You Need to Advocate for Your Child

Schools often fall into their old way of doing things. As regards special education, the schools have fallen into such a rut of doing what they do in the way in which they do it that parents still need to advocate for an appropriate education for their child in spite of legislation and a history of revised special education law.

From the initial act (Public Law 94-142), the law has been revised and renamed over the years. The Individuals with Disabilities Education Act was originally known as the Education of All Handicapped Children Act of 1975. The initial focus was to provide due process procedures and protections to children with disabilities. While retaining the procedural safeguards, the focus has now shifted to improving the educational outcomes for all children with disabilities with a new title <u>No Child Left Behind.</u>

Legislation usually becomes enforced when there is a grass roots effort to claim the rights legislated into law. So, a representative grass roots effort would be individual parents within a school or school district doing as a group what this document recommends that you do as a parent—advocate for your child.

There are six key ingredients to being an effective advocate:

Learn the rules—

·   Study the laws and educate yourselves about your local school district

·   Create relationships with school staff

·   Know how decisions are made and by whom

·   Know about the child's and your own legal rights

·   Know that a child with a disability is entitled to an "appropriate" education

·   Know that a child with a disability is not necessarily entitled to the "best" education or one that "maximizes" his or her potential, but one that is "appropriate" for his specific needs

·   Know the procedures you must follow to protect the child's rights

Plan and prepare—

·   Find out about rights and responsibilities

·   Read special education laws, regulations and cases

·   Be self-confident and committed to the child's best interests

·   Learn how to use test scores to monitor a child's progress (the school psychologist might be helpful)

·   Prepare for meetings, create agendas, write objectives and use meeting worksheets and follow-up letters to clarify problems and get to the agreement phase.

Keep written records—

·   Make requests in writing

·   Write polite follow-up letters to document events, discussions, and meetings.

Ask questions and listen carefully—

·   Use "Who, What, Why, Where, When, How" questions when you are trying to find out reasons for the school's decision(s) about giving services or other problems

Identify problems and list solutions—

·   Be sure to define and describe problems adequately

·   Use your knowledge base, feelings and past experiences to help you develop and hone strategies

·   Use basic computer skills and/or Internet skills to help you gain the information that you may need

Propose solutions—

·   Negotiate with the school for special education services

·   Always discuss issues and make offers or proposals to come up with "win-win" solutions that may be satisfactory to the child and the school. Use meeting time effectively and then follow up.[xxxv]

To empower the group—

·   Educate each other regarding your rights.

·   Clarify the question "Is special education appropriate even if the child is eligible?" (Special education is not always an "appropriate" instructional alternative. Modifications and accommodations in the general education classroom is the least restrictive alternative).

·   Understand the question "What information does your assessment provide that will assist us in designing classroom interventions?" (Remember that you need to know specific strengths and weaknesses in your child's learning skills.)

Even if you don't have an assessment of specific behaviors the school is complaining about something, look on the internet, find an intervention for whatever they say is the reason for referral for assessment, and say "let's try this first." These activities are appropriate at any point in the process from assessment, through the development of the IEP to long-term placement.

When Special Education Has Not Made a Difference

It is assumed here that you have tried everything else and have given consent for your child to receive a "special" education. If the "special" education was appropriate, your learning-disabled child should be showing evidence of improvement by the second semester. If he has been in special education for a while and remains at the same achievement level, the "special" education program is not "appropriate" and you should be monitoring closely to find out why.

Experts in the field say that all children can learn. Even the most severely mentally handicapped child can learn social skills. Surely a child with average intelligence can learn. It just takes a lot of time and effort and exploration with different instructional methods to discover how to best facilitate his individual learning style.

When you have attended all the meetings, asked all the questions, advocated to the best of your ability and your child is still not learning, it is time to take action.

Purchase a three-hole punch and a three ring binder and store all your documents and report cards in one place. Get a copy of everything in your child's cumulative folder and keep it with the other documents in your three-ring binder. You will want all the evidence they are using to make a decision about your child. Keep careful records, including observations reported by your child's teachers and any communications between home and school (notes, reports, letters, etc. and document phone calls). Then, if you have to go to a hearing or to court regarding the matter of your child's legal right to an appropriate education, you will be well-prepared when your attorney requests documentation.

Then you have the option of withdrawing your child and enrolling him/her in a school with a good reputation for providing educational services to children with special needs. When it has been demonstrated that your child has learned when enrolled in an "appropriate" program, you can sue your old school district. Precedent cases suggest that the school district will have to repay all your tuition costs and other expenses.

There are multiple sources of free information available on the Internet through foundations and government-funded agencies, which will assist you with this process. Read several pages, looking for advocacy organizations that provide educational information for parents. If you have questions, you can email them and they will respond with an answer. Here is a sample direct from the web pages:

www.ldonline.org LD Online is a national educational service of public television station WETA in Washington, D.C. The Web page features thousands of helpful articles on learning disabilities and ADHD, monthly columns by noted experts in the field, a free and confidential question and answer service, active bulletin boards and a Yellow Pages referral directory of professionals, schools, and products.

www.seirweb.com *Special Education Resources on the Internet (SERI) is a collection of Internet-accessible information resources of interest to those involved in the fields related to special education. This collection exists in order to make online special education resources more easily and readily available in one location. This site will continually modify, update and add additional informative links.*

www.ncld.org National Center for Learning Disabilities (NCLD) works to ensure that the nation's 15 million children, adolescents and adults with learning disabilities have every opportunity to succeed in school, work and life. They provide essential information to parents, professionals and individuals with learning disabilities, promote research and programs to foster effective learning, and advocate for policies to protect and strengthen educational rights and opportunities.

www.allkindsofminds.org All Kinds of Minds is a non-profit institute dedicated to the understanding of differences in learning. The Institute offers professional development for K-12 educators and helps families understand why a student is struggling in school. It was founded in 1995 to translate the latest research on how children learn into programs, products and services that help struggling students become more successful learners. Co-founded and co-chaired by Dr. Mel Levine and Charles Swab of SwabLearning.org.

www.schwablearning.org Schwab Learning is a nonprofit program of the Charles and Helen Schwab Foundation. Their mission is to provide information and inspiration for families whose children struggle with learning and attention problems.

www.pbs.org/wgbh/misunderstoodminds This site is a companion to the PBS special Misunderstood Minds, Public Broadcasting System WGBH and profiles a variety of learning problems and expert opinions. It is designed to give parents and teachers a better understanding of learning processes, insights into difficulties, and strategies for responding.

www.helpforfamilies.com Help for Families is a parenting resource for families of preschool- to middle school-age children. The site is prepared by Timothy Dunnigan, Ph.D.

www.wrightslaw.com Wrightslaw provides accurate, up-to-date information about special education law and advocacy for children with disabilities. You will find articles, cases, newsletters and resources about dozens of topics in the Advocacy and Law Libraries. This Web page is highly recommended for anyone who plans to become a serious advocate for his/her child. They tell you how to do it over the long haul all the way to the Supreme Court.

www.optometristsnetwork.org Optometrists Network provides

information on Developmental Delays, Vision Therapy and learning-related Visual Problems.

www.ilt.co.za Integrative Learning Therapy brings together knowledge and practice from various fields. These include neurophysiology, cognitive psychology and sensory integration and nutrition. ILT uses this knowledge to help overcome problems associated with learning and the demands of living. As such, their approach is eco-systemic. It considers everything within the individual and his/her environment that may be a factor causing learning or behavior difficulties.

www.handle.org The HANDLE Institute provides an effective, non-drug alternative for identifying and treating most neurodevelopmental disorders across the lifespan including Autism, ADD, ADHD, Dyslexia and Tourette's Syndrome. HANDLE incorporates research and techniques from many disciplines. It includes principles and perspectives from medicine, rehabilitation, psychology, education and nutrition. It is founded on an interactive, developmental model of human functioning. The HANDLE Institute International, LLC offers clinical services, community information, and professional training programs.

CHAPTER XII

TESTS AND TESTING

The Individuals with Disabilities Education Act (IDEA) requires parental participation in all identification and assessment processes that are primarily based upon testing. IDEA assumes that parental involvement in the education of children improves the well-being of families, enhances parenting skills, and improves educational results for children.

As a consequence, IDEA has mandated parental involvement throughout the special education process. The parental role includes giving permission to test, approval of tests to be used, provision of background information that will assist in the interpretation of test results and determining eligibility and program design.

Testing helps the teacher and other IEP team members determine potential strengths and weaknesses and current performance levels. There are many types of assessments, however, this chapter will be concerned with intelligence testing, which is utilized to predict learning potential and achievement testing, which measures what the child has learned. Together, the results from these two tests help to determine whether the child is reaching his potential for achievement. This information provides insight for appropriate educational programming.

Intelligence Testing

For the past 50 years, the general intelligence approach defined by the Wechsler Intelligence Scale for Children (WISC) has been the standard for intelligence testing, dominating the field of intellectual assessment. As a result, most professionals in education and psychology readily accept that there are two types of intelligence—verbal and non-verbal.

When interpreting the test, the verbal score indicates the child's skill with words and language and the performance score indicates primarily visual-motor or non-verbal skills. These two, when combined, result in the overall Full Scale IQ.

In the case of a significant difference of 15 points or more between the scores, the lower performance score will be a reflection of weaker visual motor skills. When this occurs, the performance score may be low enough that when added to the verbal score, the overall IQ falls below the average range (85 – 115). If this is the case, the verbal score is deemed to be a better indicator of your child's cognitive abilities than the overall IQ.

For decades, learning disabilities have been diagnosed using this IQ-achievement discrepancy model. According to this model, children whose achievement scores are a standard deviation or more below their average IQ scores (or significantly higher verbal score) are identified as learning disabled. However, this method of identifying learning disabilities and the use of IQ tests is being challenged. A recent report of the President's Commission on Excellence in Special Education, for example, makes a definitive statement about whether we should be using IQ tests for educational purposes. The commission suggests that the use of intelligence tests to diagnose learning disabilities should be discontinued.

Recent Research

New research supporting the Commission's finding indicates that the WISC IQ, which reflects achievement and culture, is not the best way to determine a child's ability to learn. Additionally, the literature suggests that the WISC discriminates against African-American children and children whose primary language is not English. These two groups have been over-represented as having cognitive deficits (mentally retarded) when tested on the WISC.

Discrimination aside, the consequence for all children is that the individual subtest scores provided by the WISC do not provide the specific information needed to begin to design an appropriate educational program. Verbal and performance scores on the WISC suggest that language-related skills may be weaker or stronger than non-language problem-solving skills, but it does not begin to tell you where those strengths and weakness lie so that they can be utilized in classroom planning.

In the past 15 years, there have been new comers to the field, including the Kaufman Assessment Battery for Children (K-ABC) and the Cognitive Assessment System (CAS). The authors of these instruments have become interested in clarifying a new way of looking at intelligence as it relates to how children learn.

Luria, a Soviet scholar, is perhaps the leading cognitive and neuro-psychological researcher to have influenced test developers. His works have helped stimulate an increased awareness of the relationships between human performance and how one learns, thereby influencing what is considered to be intelligence and how to measure it.

The Kaufman Assessment Battery for Children (K-ABC) was the first test influenced by Luria's cognitive processing theory of human functioning, but it was not designed to measure his four processes specifically. The K-ABC was based on two very important concepts. First, that verbal IQ is not intelligence, but rather reflects achievement. Second, that intelligence is best redefined as how one learns and applies information in problem solving.

The Cognitive Assessment System is also based largely on the neuropsychological work of Luria. The PASS theory (Planning, Attention,

Simultaneous Processing, and Successive Processing) was formulated into a test that puts emphasis on basic psychological processes that are related to performance. The author states that PASS cognitive processes or abilities interact with an individual's base of knowledge and skills. The four constructs of the test and their functions suggest that:

·   **Planning** is critical to all activities in which the child or adult has to determine how to solve a problem.

·   **Attention** is a mental process by which a child is able to focus on particular stimuli, and ignore all other competing stimuli.

·   **Simultaneous Processing** is the need to recognize how the multiple parts of a stimulus are interrelated into a whole.

·   **Successive Processing** is required when a person must arrange things in a strictly defined order where each element is only related to those that precede it.

Although individual tasks may require the integration of all these processes, not every process is equally involved in every task. For example, tests like math calculation may be heavily weighted or influenced, by a single PASS process such as planning, while decoding in reading is strongly related to successive processing. Because the processes are inter-related in achievement and learning, a thorough understanding of a child's competence in all these areas is important for addressing educational problems.

The four PASS scales represent the kinds of basic psychological processes that are used in the Individuals with Disabilities Education Act Amendments of 1997 to define a learning disability. These four basic psychological processes can be used to discover strengths and weaknesses of children, which can then be used for effective differential diagnosis, planning for classroom instruction and to select or design appropriate interventions.

In order to help the child learn, it is important to match instruction to the cognitive strengths of the child, while developing weaknesses. The CAS comes closest to meeting this need by merging the best in psychometric test development methods with a theory of intelligence as how one learns and then placing emphasis on basic psychological processes that are related to performance. Additionally, the authors have identified and made available specific classroom interventions and instructional methods that address specific strengths and weaknesses identified by the test.[xxi]i

The Differential Ability Scales (DAS) improves significantly upon the Wechsler as an intelligence test that measures cognitive ability. The DAS assumes each person to have a certain general level of intellectual ability that can be demonstrated in most areas of problem-solving, although it will be expressed differently under different circumstances. This general or global intelligence is commonly referred to by the single italicized letter *g*. The DAS uses the terms "psychometric *g*" and General Conceptual Ability (GCA) instead of IQ.

Having used the DAS exclusively for one year, this author found it to be preferable to the Wechsler in that it provides information regarding spatial abilities, factors out some other areas and includes an achievement test for better comparison with the GCA. However, it is, as stated by its author, a measure of cognitive ability that translates to intelligence and GCA, which translates to the old IQ. It is in essence an intelligence test and, with the exception of a spatial component, it does not identify specific learning strengths and weaknesses. Like the Wechsler, it is difficult to translate findings into interventions or classroom planning.

Individual Tests of Academic Achievement

The discrepancy between ability and achievement, the second eligibility requirement for special education, is determined through the administration of an individual achievement test. While there are many tests available, the Woodcock- Johnson Psycho-Educational Battery-III Tests of Achievement, commonly referred to as the Woodcock-Johnson, is one of the primary diagnostic tools used by evaluators to determine whether a student has learning disabilities.

Designed to measure intellectual abilities and academic achievement, the Woodcock-Johnson is equally as appropriate for individuals age 2 to 90. It assesses Reading, Oral Language, Mathematics, Written Language, Knowledge, Supplemental Scores, Intra-Achievement Discrepancies and Total Achievement, in an administration time of 60 to 70 minutes.

The Woodcock Johnson III-Tests of Achievement (WJ III ACH) updates and expands the Revised Version with the intention of improving the diagnostic power of the instrument. It is designed to identify and describe an individual's current strengths and weaknesses. Three oral tests, a diagnostic spelling test and a measure of phonological awareness have been added to evaluate fluency in reading and in math.

The second battery, the WJ III Test of Cognitive Abilities (WJ III COG), is designed to measure general and specific cognitive functions. When these two batteries are administered together, they allow the tester to investigate over-underachievement and to examine patterns of discrepancies among cognitive or achievement areas.

Subtests in the Cognitive Battery measure memory for names and sentences, identification of pictures and logic. The Achievement Battery contains tests of passage comprehension, calculation, science, social studies, a writing sample and other school-related topics. Of particular importance for evaluating a dyslexic student are several supplemental Woodcock-Johnson tests: Sound Blending, Sound Patterns, Letter-Word Identification and Word Attack.

Phonological Awareness

Phonological awareness is one of the best predictors of early reading acquisition—better than IQ, vocabulary or listening comprehension. As such, it is an important predictor of educational achievement. Deficits in this area are a major cause of severe reading problems.

Phonological awareness is the ability to focus on the sound structure of language, apart from its meaning. To learn to read and spell, we must attend to the relationship between the sounds and the letters of language. This knowledge of sound-symbol relationships is a key to reading and understanding written language.

The *WJ III* contains five tests that measure different aspects of phonological awareness. In fact, the *WJ III Tests of Cognitive Abilities* is presently the only major intelligence test that measures auditory processing and phonemic awareness. The cognitive battery contains Sound Blending, which requires a subject to blend speech sounds to form a word, and

Incomplete Words, which requires a subject to analyze a word with missing sounds and identify the complete word.

In the *WJ III Tests of Achievement*, three tests measure aspects of phonological awareness. Examiners can use Word Attack and Spelling of Sounds to assess a subject's sound/symbol knowledge and determine if the subject can apply both the sound of words and correct sequences and configuration of letters to identify and spell words. And if further analysis is needed, examiners can use Sound Awareness to measure a subject's ability to rhyme words and manipulate phonemes.

What Does This Mean for My Child

If a student with learning disabilities is of "average" or "above average" intelligence, the cognitive portion of the Woodcock-Johnson test will point out strengths in academic functioning that will not show up in the achievement portion of the test. A student with learning disabilities often scores high in oral language and verbal ability. This is the individual whose intelligence and strengths are displayed in conversation with others. This student is usually so skillful verbally that the general public never suspects a learning disability. A student can score low in math on the achievement portion of the test, yet score high in the reasoning areas of the cognitive test. A high score in reasoning areas indicates good potential in math reasoning skills as well.

Test results on the cognitive portion combined with the achievement portion of the Woodcock-Johnson indicate the "learning style" of a student with learning disabilities. A student who does poorly on the visual subtests, yet scores high on auditory subtests, is probably an auditory learner.

The Visual Perceptual Speed Score on the cognitive portion of the Woodcock-Johnson can indicate possible visual perceptual problems, which signal the need for further in- depth testing of visual skills.

If assessments include both the achievement and cognitive portions of the Woodcock-Johnson Psychoeducational Battery, the assessment will provide a realistic analysis of strengths and weaknesses as well as an insight into some of the learning disabilities that make learning so difficult.

Coping with learning disabilities begins with analysis of the problems. The Woodcock-Johnson Battery, when given in its complete form, is a hopeful beginning to understanding the strengths and weaknesses that require modification and accommodation in the classroom.[xxii]i

Tests of Visual-Motor Integration

The tests most often used to identify problems with visual-motor integration in educational assessments are the Beery-Buktenica Developmental Test of Visual-Motor Integration (Beery VMI) and the Bender Visual-Motor Gestalt Test.

The publishers state that the Beery VMI, now in its fifth edition, offers a convenient and economical way to *screen* for visual-motor deficits that can lead to learning and behavioral problems. This test helps assess the extent to which individuals can integrate their visual and motor abilities by asking the individual to copy drawings of geometric forms, arranged in order of increasing difficulty, into an accompanying space.

This instrument does not provide much information about the nature of the child's disability; rather, it compares his performance with that of other children and provides an age- equivalent score (the average age of other children with the same score), as well as an overall standard score for performance (which can be compared with his performance score on the WISC). If the child is 10 and receives an age- equivalent score of 7, this means that he is functioning at the developmental level of a 7-year-old. This gives a clue as to how to modify the classroom and instruction. He may be in the fourth or fifth grade, but his eyes and fine motor skills are only ready for second- or third-grade work.

The other instrument used to assess this area is the Bender Visual-Motor Gestalt Test, a classic measure of visual-motor integration. This instrument has been updated into a second edition and continues its tradition as a brief test of visual-motor integration that may provide information about an individual's development and psychological functioning.

The test is a valuable aid in the diagnosis of learning problems, emotional disturbances and neurological malfunctioning. It also serves as a predictor of achievement among elementary school pupils. The test provides a maximum amount of information in a minimal time of 12 minutes.

While both the Beery VMI and the Bender Gestalt assess one's ability to copy designs using paper and pencil, the Bender Gestalt is more challenging in that it requires the child to organize his work on a blank piece of paper. It provides information regarding perseveration, orientation in space, visual closure and other interpretive information. Parents should insist upon the use of this test because of the extensive specific interpretative data, which will assist in the development of classroom interventions appropriate for the individual child.

Psycho-Educational Assessment

Contrary to what you may believe, the purpose of the School Psychologist's assessment is not to diagnose learning strengths and weaknesses; rather, it is to determine whether or not the child meets the eligibility criteria for special education. Eligibility for special education is determined by the discrepancy model, which requires that there be a processing disorder along with one standard deviation of difference between ability and achievement. Therefore, as mandated by law, school assessments emphasize identification of a discrepancy and a processing disorder. Learning strengths and weaknesses as needed for educational planning is not part of the special education assessment.

While the role of the school psychologist may differ slightly from state to state, they cannot do more than the law allows them to do in terms of assessment. Therefore, remaining consistent with the law, the school psychologist's training, which may also differ from one university to another, emphasizes the development of expertise with those instruments utilized to meet the dictates of the law.

Additionally, they are limited to the use of instruments purchased and provided by the school district that employs them. Assessment instruments are very expensive and most school districts purchase only those instruments needed to meet the objective of determining eligibility for special education. Most other instruments, not being relevant to the determination of eligibility for special education, are not routinely purchased by school districts.

The question then becomes, "How do you get your school district to purchase the test instruments that will identify your child's learning strengths and weaknesses?"

What to Do

It is unfortunate that the identification of specific strengths and weaknesses, which would be helpful in designing an appropriate educational program, is not an integral part of every public school psycho-educational assessment. It should become so and you, and perhaps your friends or advocacy group, can accomplish this objective gradually in every meeting you attend by asking the school psychologist and the resource specialist this very impressive question:

"What information does your assessment provide that will assist us in designing classroom interventions? I am particularly interested in identified strengths and weaknesses which can be used to design classroom intervention, and/or design an appropriate instructional program."

Remember! Special education can be considered when everything else has been tried without success. Even if special education seems an appropriate placement for the child, this specific information is needed more than ever so that the child's special education will not only be "special," but "appropriate" as well.

When you demonstrate that you are an informed parent with the question: "what information does your assessment provide that will assist us in designing classroom interventions?" there will be many long explanations about the training of special education teachers and the qualified resource specialist at your child's school, but the reality of the situation is that they don't know, from the school psychologist's evaluation, what to do to help your child to learn. This is particularly true if the Wechsler Intelligence Scale for Children was used in the assessment.

To design an appropriate educational program, it takes a diagnosis of the specific nature of a disability and how it manifests in strengths and weaknesses in the individual child. Without knowledge of specific strengths and weaknesses, the special education teacher may come closer to designing a relevant program, but neither teacher will come close to designing an "appropriate" one. That is why your learning-handicapped child will not come any closer to achieving his potential in special education than he will in the general education classroom.

In order to know how to accommodate your child's learning problem in the general education classroom, you need to know the exact nature of your child's learning problem and while that should be the purpose of the psychoeducational assessment, it isn't. Therefore, you will have to ask your very impressive question regarding what the assessment offers in terms of "specific strengths and weaknesses" until someone begins to identify them to your satisfaction.

Parents and teachers who refer a student to a school study team for assessment should request, and if necessary insist, that both the cognitive and achievement portions of the Woodcock-Johnson test be administered. Often, only the achievement portion is given, which points out the student's academic weaknesses.

The cognitive test of the Woodcock Johnson also needs to be given to provide a more complete picture of the student's academic functioning. The combination of both the cognitive and the achievement test results give valuable information concerning the strengths and weaknesses of the student, the student's learning style, the possible presence of visual perceptual difficulties and the student's aptitude in academic areas.

If the WISC was used to determine IQ, you have the right to request the use of one of the newer instruments, like the Cognitive Assessment System or the Woodcock-Johnson *Tests of Cognitive Abilities, or both the cognitive and achievement tests of the Woodcock Johnson.* Together these tests give you a complete picture of psychoneurological development.

Having used these tests for years, this author would prefer the CAS, which measures constructs more closely related to classroom performance, and the Woodcock-Johnson Achievement and Cognitive Batteries for identification of strengths and weaknesses. However, the Woodcock-Johnson is designed for use by professionals. Classroom interventions are not provided.

For the skilled examiner, the Achievement and Cognitive Batteries of the Woodcock-Johnson provide the most comprehensive insight into the strengths and weaknesses of children. Add to this the findings from the Bender Gestalt for visual-motor function and you should have a complete picture of a child's psychoeducational needs.

Then finally, remind yourself that you are not out to change the educational system—only the way that your child experiences it. You are an advocate for one child—yours.

CHAPTER XIII

ADVOCACY AT ITS BEST

As stated previously, before beginning advocacy for your child's education, it would be helpful to be sure that you have addressed any trauma, injuries, nutritional or health problems and had his vision and hearing checked so that you are assured that you are doing or have done your part at home to prepare your child for learning. The goal is to ensure that what you are going to ask the schools to do is a complement to all the work that has been done at home in preparing your child to learn; not a substitute for any work that should have been done.

Special education was enacted by the Federal Government to provide "special" educational programming for disabled or "special needs" children. It was called "special" because it differed from the general education program provided for everyone else. By definition, special education is an educational program that modifies the learning environment through special teaching techniques, classroom modifications, assistive learning devices, individualized instruction and smaller class sizes.

Because children with learning disabilities represent the largest category of students receiving special education, the term has become so closely associated with special education that some professionals have actually referred to special education as a form of treatment for learning disabilities. However, this is far from the truth of what special education is and does.

Special education does not "treat" learning or any other problem associated with the central nervous system. Your child's learning disability will not eventually go away if he enters special education. When a child has a learning problem, the special classroom modifies the way the information is presented to the child. If his problem is visual processing, information may be presented so that the stronger auditory channels are utilized. The child then learns more effectively, but that does not mean that the visual processing problem has been treated or cured.

Children with many types of neurological (brain) immaturity benefit from the special assistance they receive in special education. Switching learning modalities (visual to the stronger auditory) early in the child's learning experience assists him in learning the basics early so that he does not fall too far behind in acquiring the building blocks for reading or math.

For this reason, it is recommended that your child's disability be diagnosed early and intervention started. This means to identify and address the environmental problem contributing to the disability and get any needed professional help. The degree of recovery is dependent upon the severity of the trauma, the ability to modify the child's environment and the relationship the parent has with the child.

The law states that identification should occur at an early age and that services should be provided in the least restrictive environment. This means that instruction should occur in the general education classroom whenever possible. Removal from the general education classroom should be a last resort, used only after the child has received a specialized assessment to determine his strengths and weaknesses and everything in the way of modification and accommodation has been tried.

Learning-disabled children by definition have average or above-average intelligence. That means that they have the ability to learn and have learned what they have been exposed to at the same level as other children their age.

The only difference between a learning-disabled child and another child is his ability to benefit from the teaching methods utilized in the general education classroom. This translates to mean underachievement, resulting from the fact that the child does not benefit from the routine teaching methods that have historically been utilized in our schools. The learning-disabled child may require more emphasis on visual presentation, more emphasis on auditory information or a kinesthetic approach.

This means that learning-disabled children do not learn in the same way that the majority of children learn and that assessment is needed to assist the teacher in identifying how to accommodate their individualized needs. Without this help, the teacher is overwhelmed with challenges for which she may have been ill-prepared in her training program. Add to that an overcrowded classroom of 30 to 35 students and the special needs of the child that is different often go unmet.

When this scenario exists, the child with a different learning style is often referred to special education, where the smaller class size is expected to make it easier to implement the accommodations and modifications needed to help him/her to learn. However, while this may be the hype surrounding special education, it is seldom the experience of the learning- disabled child with average intelligence who has been isolated from the general education classroom.

Approval for the placement of your child in an isolated group should be given only after you have visited the class, examined the curriculum and talked with the teacher about special teaching techniques, because all classrooms for a specific learning disability are not created equal.

Some special classes are appropriate, with highly qualified teachers instructing them. However, some smaller settings for children with a specific learning disability are dumping grounds for hard-to-instruct children and the teachers are not of the best caliber. In the 20-year career of this writer, the curriculum was found to be unchallenging, individual learning styles were not accommodated and the children complained of not learning anything. At re-evaluation many have begged to be returned to their regular classrooms.

IDEA legislation and regulations require that, to the maximum extent appropriate, students with disabilities must be educated with their non-disabled peers. However, data suggests that students with disabilities living in inner-cities are more likely to be placed in restrictive learning environments. In these settings, 41.3 percent of students with disabilities are enrolled in full-time programs that remove students from regular classes for 50 percent or more of the school day, compared to 23.4 percent in non-inner-city areas.

Once placed in these classes, without specific assessment and accommodation of their learning style, they continue to underachieve. As a consequence, they are rarely able to return to an educational setting with their non-disabled peers because they have fallen too far behind academically and are, therefore, condemned to these settings for the remainder of their school experience. Eventually, because school is so meaningless, by middle school truancy becomes a problem and they drop out.

This raises a question: If the child is not going to learn at grade level anyway, why is it that he cannot be accommodated in the general education classroom and at least learn the social skills available through interaction with his classmates? The answer is that teachers sometimes believe the hype given to parents. "He will benefit more from placement in special education." And theoretically that should be true, but in reality it often is not.

Again, the school district has a logical defense for its actions. It is hard to retain good teachers in some schools where there is limited parental participation; there are a limited number of English-speaking students, etc. However, that is not a problem with which you will be concerned. Your objective is to see that your child receives an appropriate education. And if an appropriate education cannot be provided in his home school environment, see that he is transported to an environment in which he can receive an appropriate education. And if English is not his primary language, see that he is enrolled in a class that will develop his academic skills while he is learning English.

What You May Not Know about

Your Child's Referral for Special Education

Part of the reason for referral to special education is that your child may present a problem for the classroom teacher because he/she has to work harder to accommodate your child's unique learning style and he/she would rather not work that hard. So the teacher gets rid of the demand upon her time by referring the child in need to special education. "I want that child out of my classroom" was not infrequently heard around public schools.

Another reason is that in order to have a resource specialist program in a school, a minimum number of students needing the services is required. Now, let's suppose the number in your state is 12 and there are only 10 students identified. If that resource specialist or special day class teacher wants to keep her position in the school where she has taught for years and where all her friends are, that teacher is likely to be motivated to find two additional students so she can keep her job or so that the class can stay at that school.

It may be a coincidence, but one of the students referred to special education might be your child. So, an additional question becomes, does my child "need" special education and is special education "appropriate" for my child even if he is eligible? If English is not his primary language, he should not be considered for special education unless he was assessed in his primary language and has had an opportunity to participate in English as a Second Language class.

The answer to these two questions will be revealed as you go through the process of determining eligibility for special education. With good advocacy you can weather this storm and achieve an educational program that is "appropriate" for your child in "the least restrictive learning environment." It is your right under the law. And with good advocacy and involvement in the process, you can claim your rights.

The Process of Determining Eligibility

The first thing that will relieve your mind and/or concerns about your child's need for a "special" education is that you are in the driver's seat. Federal and state laws made you the controlling factor in the entire process. The parent's "informed consent" is required at every step of the process, start to finish. This means that you can go through the assessment process without any obligation to agree to placement in special education. Even through your child may be found eligible the school district cannot place him in special education without your agreement in the form of your signature. If you don't agree, don't sign the IEP until you have what you consider to be an "appropriate" educational placement and individualized education plan.

The process begins when the classroom teacher notices that your child is not doing as well academically as most of his peers. After careful review of the teacher's comments, you are invited to meet with the student study team all his teachers and others share with you how your child is doing. Following a lengthy discussion of how you child is doing academically and behaviorally, you may be asked to give permission for your child to be assessed to determine how best to modify his educational program to facilitate learning.

If you decide to go further with the exploration of your child's learning problems, you will be asked to sign an assessment plan, which gives the school district permission to administer a series of standardized tests to determine your child's skills and abilities. If this has all come as a shock to you and you don't like the way things are going, don't sign the permission form. Nothing can be done until you do. They may continue to call and send forms, but a reply such as, "I am looking further into this matter of special education" should satisfy them for a while.

After you have done your research and tried all the things suggested in this book, you can always find the form and sign it, or ask them to send you another one. They started the process and now you are in control. Once the papers are signed, they have 65 days (it may vary from state to state) to get the process started; you can still change your mind again if something new happens. Remember, you are in the driver's seat; they have to follow the law, which says they can't do anything until you give your permission.

If you have given permission, the tests are completed and the child has been determined to be eligible, you will again be invited to the school to hear the results and write an Individualized Education Plan (IEP).

In this meeting you will be told whether your child has average, above-average or below-average cognitive ability, which suggests the rate at which he should be able to learn when compared with other students his age. In addition, you will be informed that there is a discrepancy between what the cognitive ability (intelligence) test says he should be able to do and what he did on an individual achievement test. If there is a significant difference of 15 points between these two scores, your child has met the first criterion of eligibility for special education.

Next, it has to be determined why this difference between scores exists. Based upon the results of a number of tests the school psychologist gave your child, it may be concluded that the difference is due to a "processing" problem. If your child doesn't follow instructions because he can't hear the teacher's voice over the noise in the classroom, it is assumed that he/she fails to learn because of an "auditory processing problem." If he can't read because he can't focus on the page, he is determined to have a "visual processing problem." If his writing is poor and he writes off the end of the page or doesn't write on the lines, he is determined to have a "visual-motor problem," etc.

Maybe you have noticed some of these behaviors at home when compared with his siblings or other children in the neighborhood. Or you have always been suspicious that something was wrong because it takes forever for him to complete his homework, even with your help. So you say in the meeting, "I have noticed those things also and he certainly needs some kind of help"—so you decide to sign the papers so your child can begin his "special" education.

Why You Didn't Have Informed Consent

Prior to signing the papers, you should have been "informed" that special education was not your only option. The law states that you child is entitled to a "free, appropriate, public education" and that services should be provided in the "least restrictive environment." This means that instruction should occur in the general education classroom whenever possible, should be in a language that your child can understand, is appropriate for your child's needs, and leads to some form of learning which can be construed as an "education."

According to the law, telling you about your child's identified learning problem is not the end of the school's responsibility. You should be told of all the options available to address his learning needs, the need for visual and auditory examination, his learning strengths and weaknesses and how they can be addressed with trial modifications and accommodations in the general education classroom to determine if there is a "need" for segregation into a "special" setting.

Because most information in the classroom requires either good visual or auditory skills, the law states that a child should have a visual and/or auditory evaluation before being placed in special education. This means that if the child evidences problems with hearing, the school district should test his hearing. If he has problems with vision, his vision should be tested.

You will likely be told in a meeting that the nurse checked his vision and his vision is normal. This means that he could see, at twenty feet, the Es or other objects of various sizes on a Snellen, or some other chart used to test the vision of children.

What you were not informed of is that there is a great deal of difference between being able to see the big E on a Snellen chart at 20 feet in the nurse's office and being able to see the print of a textbook 18 inches from his face. When they tell you that they checked your child's vision and it is normal, that may be pretty far from the truth of the matter. The fact may be that your child has problems with visual-motor integration, poor near vision or poor eye coordination. None of these, including near vision, is checked during a school vision exam. There may be exceptions to this, but it is certainly not a very large exception.

School districts don't exactly lie to parents; but in all the school districts in which this writer has worked, there was a policy to tell parents as little as possible about their child's problem. It was generally stated in this manner: "If we tell parents that their child needs his eyes examined, we by law are required to pay for the examination. If we don't tell them, we don't have to pay."

Again, the school district is not exactly lying; they simply are not sharing everything that they know. Schools are forced into this little subterfuge because when the legislature wrote the laws, they did not provide any funds for the schools to use to implement them. So school officials, out of a need to keep the school doors open, have just opted not to address the question of why the child isn't seeing properly. Instead, they tell parents that the child has a visual processing problem and special education is the answer.

Examination of visual, auditory, language and visual-motor problems was mandated because the legislature acknowledged that the information was needed in order to design an appropriate educational program for special-needs children. The fact that they did not allocate funds with which to do it did not negate the fact that it needs to be done.

Additionally, your child may have a specific learning problem that does not appear to be evident when assessed by the school psychologist. Remember that school psychologists in most areas are psychometricians (who administer tests), not diagnosticians (who determine causes). Because there are many disabling conditions that the school psychologist is not trained to identify, it may become necessary for you to get an outside evaluation to pinpoint the specific needs of your child. A child whose problem is due primarily to a visual problem correctable with glasses is not eligible for special education. A child who is deaf or hard of hearing is not classified as having a learning disability. The exact nature of the problem has to be identified in order to design an appropriate program.

Designing an Appropriate

Individualized Education Plan

There are two approaches used by schools to meet the needs of children with special learning needs. The first is to make changes in the physical space in the classroom itself, known as modifications, and the second is changes in teaching methods, known as accommodations. This simply means that the teacher changes where the student is physically located within the classroom and takes into consideration his learning strengths when teaching him. If auditory processing is the area of weakness, then teaching materials are prepared so that the stronger visual skills are used for learning.

The IEP team should first determine what modifications can be made without removing the child from the classroom, because the resource specialist can come to the regular classroom to provide assistance with instruction (this should be written into the IEP). The only time you might want to consider removal to the resource specialist program is when, because of developmental immaturity, the child has not learned skills presented in earlier grades. Be sure that the IEP states "development of basic skills not learned in earlier grades."

If you have been properly informed, you may choose to consent to a smaller setting, with individualized instruction, after everything else has been tried. However, for our purposes we are concerned with the development of an instructional program that is "appropriate," meaning classroom instruction that utilizes the student's learning strengths, while strengthening weaknesses in the least restrictive environment. And an "appropriate" Individual Education Plan cannot be written until you know what those strengths and weaknesses are.

Failure occurs for four reasons that should be examined during the assessment process:

- Environmentally caused trauma has not been removed or addressed
- Specific strengths and weaknesses have not been identified
- Appropriate accommodations and modifications have not been established
- The pace of the instruction is too rapid for the child to achieve mastery of skills presented.

Questions To Ask During the IEP

If the child was assessed with the WISC, ask that he be assessed on an instrument like the CAS or both batteries of the Woodcock-Johnson. (These tests are explained in the chapter entitled Tests and Testing).

- Is there any environmentally caused trauma that may be interfering with achievement?
- Is assistance available to address any environmental trauma, would a mentor help?
- What are my child's specific strengths and weaknesses?
- Are there specific therapies and interventions available to address his developmental needs?
- What interventions or therapies are available at school and what others does the school support or recommend?
- Has it been determined that my child does not have a visual or hearing problem? (You may have to get the evaluation yourself, but it is really their responsibility. The school nurse's test is not sufficient.)
- Is he an auditory or visual learner?
- How will we utilize his strengths?
- What are you doing or what will be done to accommodate his

weaknesses?

- Will the resource specialist participate in the identifying needed accommodations and modifications?
- How can my child be supported at home?
- How will I be informed about my child's progress?

If you get boxed in or feel overwhelmed, call a time-out and reschedule after a time, during which you will reread and gather additional information by exploring some of the resources listed at the end of this chapter.

Having taken time out to become better informed while waiting for the test results from a new and better instrument, and having done your homework, you should request a special work session in which you will review those interventions offered and assist in designing new ones. If you have done your homework well, you may be better prepared than they are to design interventions.

After your recommended interventions have been in place for a while, you will need to follow up by scheduling a regular time to meet with the teacher, either in person or by phone, to see how the interventions are working and which ones need modification. You must ask for periodic reports of achievement and failure and encourage that they teach to your child's strengths. If he excels at math and has difficulty with English, tell them to teach him more mathematics. Academic performance has been known to improve with maturation and likely his English skills will improve with time and good intervention also.

In the real world, adults achieve in the area of their strengths; no one is expected to excel in all areas. Find out what your child can do well and nurture your child's development in that area. Don't become so focused on the weaknesses that you fail to acknowledge and develop his strengths. And above all, nurture the child's ego. Let him know that not everyone is good at everything and that when he has given his best that is the best he can give. Then remind the teacher to grade him accordingly, set the goal in that area at a level he can reach and make reaching that goal acceptable.

STOP

If there is anything that you do not completely understand about the concept of special education and how decisions are made to place your child in special education, go back and review the process. It is necessary that you understand Tests and Testing, the laws and why advocacy is sometimes needed.

A summary of important information from Part II

·   Before beginning any form of advocacy, parents should be sure that they have done their best at home to prepare the child for learning.

·   A healthy, involved relationship with his parents, good nutrition, adequate sleep and plenty of physical exercise will go a long way toward preparing a child for learning.

·   The <u>No Child Left Behind Act</u> of 2001 ensures that all children have a fair, equal and significant opportunity to obtain a high-quality education.

·   The parent's rights are numerous and far supersede those of the school district.

·   Parents still need to advocate for an appropriate education for their child in spite of legislation and a history of revised education law.

·   Parents must be proactive and take the necessary steps to make sure their child receives appropriate services.

·   Parents have the right to request that their child be assessed with a test instrument that will identify his learning strengths and weaknesses.

·   Parents have the right to know the specifics of their child's disability and how it manifests in the classroom.

·   It is recommended that a child's disability be diagnosed and intervention started early.

·   The law states that services should be provided in the least restrictive environment. This means that instruction should occur in the general education classroom whenever possible.

·   An important question to be answered: "Is special education appropriate for my child even if he is eligible?"

·   Your child cannot be placed in special education without your informed consent.

·   The IEP team should first determine what modifications can be made without removing the child from the classroom. An important question for the IEP: "What information does your assessment provide regarding learning strengths and weaknesses that will help in the design of an appropriate education for my child?"

· If your child has been in special education for a while and remains at the same achievement level, the "special" education is not "appropriate" and you should be monitoring closely to find out why.

Part III is an exploration of processing disorders usually identified as learning disabilities. This information will provide you with insight that will serve you well in your advocacy for an "appropriate" education for your child.

It will be particularly beneficial in helping you to find your own voice to communicate an informed opinion throughout the special education process. Provided are descriptions of typical behaviors exhibited in elementary, middle and high school and a rationale for an approach to designing the individualized educational plan (IEP).

CHAPTER XIV

VISUAL PROCESSING

The two most common areas of difficulty involved with a learning disability are visual and auditory processing. Since so much information in the classroom and at the home is presented visually and/or verbally, the child with an auditory or visual processing disorder is at a definite disadvantage.

A visual processing or perceptual disorder refers to a hindered ability to make sense of information that is taken in through the eyes. It is the process through which we get visual information from the environment to integrate with our other senses. Difficulties with visual processing affect how visual information is interpreted once it enters the central nervous system and can occur without impaired vision of any kind. It is not a matter of the child being able to see; the problem has to do with how the brain is able to utilize the information that is seen.

The process of vision uses more than 65% of all pathways to the brain. It takes up more brainpower than any other one thing that we do with our brain at a given time. This is because vision is not a single, solitary happening, but a whole bunch of things happening at the same time. Vision is so complicated that it involves twenty separate visual abilities. It is far more than just seeing objects clearly; it also involves processes such as how we move our eyes together, how we focus, how we perceive the world around us and how we process, store and recall information, to name just a few! This is why it is said that vision is a dynamic process—not simply one of our senses.

Most people believe that good vision only means having 20/20 acuity or seeing clearly in the distance. Schools that do vision screening usually check to see how a child's vision at 20 feet compares with what other children can see at that distance. In elementary school, children actually can see better at a distance than they can see up close. Unfortunately, what a child can see up close, at perhaps 18 inches, the distance of a book from the eyes when reading, is not often checked in a school vision exam.

This means that most children will pass a school screening but still have trouble focusing up close, remaining focused over a short period of time and/or changing their focus quickly from far to near. These skills are essential in activities such as reading fluency and copying from the board.

Facts about Vision and Learning

·   25% of all children have a vision problem significant enough to affect their performance in school.

·   This equates to 1 out of 4 children—roughly 2 to 7 million children —struggling to achieve in school.

·   By first grade all children should have had at least three vision wellness checkups: one at 6 months, one at 3 years and again before beginning school to ensure that their vision is healthy and developing normally.

·   According to the Better Vision Institute, only 14% of children have had a comprehensive vision exam by first grade!

·   As many as 80% of children who are reading-disabled, including those considered dyslexic, show a deficiency in one or more basic visual skills. [xxiii]i

Of equal importance is the fact that vision problems are almost always overlooked by parents and educators as a roadblock to learning. Here is a quick checklist of behaviors usually exhibited by children with vision-based learning problems. If five or more of these symptoms apply to your son or daughter, then your child could be one of the 20% of school-aged children who have a vision-based learning problem.

Children with Vision-based Learning Problems

May Exhibit the Following Behaviors

A Check List [xxxix]

read below grade level
have trouble comprehending
avoid reading or other close-up tasks
omit, reverse, or confuse words when reading
lose their place or use their finger to follow a line of print
become easily distracted, finding it difficult to remain on task

have a short attention span
need a lot of breaks during homework
tire quickly when they read
suffer from eye strain
have red or watery eyes when reading
complain of blurred, double or moving print
squint, frown or rub their eyes while reading
have difficulty taking tests
tilt their head at an angle or hold books too closely

when reading
cover one eye to read
have difficulty copying from the board
reverse letters and numbers (after the first grade)
fail to complete assignments on time
take a long time to do homework
appear to be unmotivated or lazy at school

seem frustrated with school

suffer from poor self-esteem

complain of headaches

struggle with eye-hand coordination

have poor handwriting

sometimes appear awkward or clumsy

have difficulty catching or hitting a ball

show symptoms of attention deficit disorder

If you found five or more of the above to be true regarding your child, a simple visit to an optometrist for a vision examination and new glasses may not be sufficient, because visual processing weaknesses may exist even with 20/20 vision. These concerns are usually addressed by a vision professional with more extensive training in the diagnosis and remediation of visual problems.

A child's comprehensive eye examination should include testing the following skills, which are all aspects of normal, healthy vision.[xl]

· Acuity-Distance: visual acuity (sharpness, clearness) at 20 feet

· Acuity-Near: visual acuity for short distance (specifically, reading distance)

· Focusing skills: the ability to maintain clear vision at varying distances

· Eye tracking and fixation skills: the ability to remain focused and move the eyes swiftly across a sheet of paper while reading, etc.

· Binocular fusion: the ability to use both eyes together and see only one object

· Stereopis: binocular depth perception

· Convergence and Eye Teaming Skills: the ability of the eyes to aim, move and work as a coordinated team

· Hyperopia: the ability to focus, especially at near viewing distances

· Color Vision: the ability to differentiate colors

· Reversal frequency: confusing letters or words (b, d; p, q; saw, was; etc.)

· Visual memory: the ability to store and retrieve visual information

·   Visual form discrimination: the ability to determine if two shapes, colors, sizes, positions or distances are the same or different

·   Visual motor integration: the ability to combine visual input with other sensory input (eye-hand movements, balance, hearing, etc.); the ability to copy images from a vertical to a horizontal plane (such as from the blackboard to the desk surface).

A Case Study[xli]

One child, as an infant, was withdrawn and could not make eye contact. By preschool she needed to smell and squeeze every object she saw. She touched faces and would bring everything to her mouth. Specialists conducted a battery of tests. Over a period of years, the possible diagnoses included: autism spectrum disorder, attention deficit disorder with hyperactivity and anxiety disorder. A behavioral pediatrician prescribed three drugs for attention deficit and depression. The only constant was that the child did anything she could to avoid reading and writing.

The results of two eye exams showed 20/20 vision, but a reading specialist suggested another examination. This time, the ophthalmologist did what no one else had done. He put his finger on the child's nose and moved it in and out. Her eyes jumped all over the place. Within minutes he had the diagnosis: convergence insufficiency, in which the patient sees double because the eyes cannot work together at close range. For this child, the treatment was relatively simple: for nine months she wore special glasses that use prisms to help the eyes converge inward. She then had three months of vision therapy. In fourth grade, at age 9, she is reading at grade level.

More Examples of Reading Difficulty

In the author's experience, there have been many children with normal intelligence and 20/20 vision who could not read. One child was asked if he could relate why he could not read and he stated that he saw two books and didn't know which one he was reading. When the child was instructed to cover one eye while reading, he demonstrated that he could read at grade level.

Other children have demonstrated an ability to see only the middle of the page, being unable to focus on the sides of the page. Some children were unable to read because they could not read across the middle of the page. When they reached the middle of the page they would lose their place because they could not make the quick transfer to the right eye, which did not work together with the left eye. Or, they moved the book back and forth as they read so that the book stayed in the range of vision of only one eye.

The thing all these children had in common is that they avoided reading and writing whenever possible. The child on the cover of this book is an example of how these children may present in the classroom. The level of frustration they suffer is experienced not only by the child, but by the classroom teacher as well. And, if you are an involved parent, you have probably experienced some frustrations of your own.

While this appears to be a visual problem, it is really a sensori-motor problem and is discussed further in the chapter entitled Sensori-Motor Integration.

Experts estimate that five percent of school children have convergence insufficiency. They can suffer headaches, dizziness and nausea, which can lead to irritability, low self-esteem and inability to concentrate. Very often, pediatricians have never heard of visual insufficiency and no consensus has been reached on how to treat it. However, for trained, qualified and experienced professionals, the training turns out to be a straightforward process. Thousands of success stories are available for your research at www.visiontherapy.org/.

You can check your child's eye muscle control at home by using these simple steps. You may remember this exercise from the end of Chapter II; it is repeated here for your convenience.

- Have the child focus on a finger held about 12 inches in front of his eyes.
- Ask the child to follow your finger with his eyes without moving his head.
- Always keep the finger the same 12 inches from his face.
- Begin at the midline (in front of his nose) and slowly move to the right side.
- Next, start at the midline and slowly move the finger to the left.

·   Carefully observe how smoothly the child is able to move his eyes.

·   If the eyes jerk back, or he loses focus, just start over.

·   Next, begin the exercise with the finger on the far right side and bring it back toward the middle and on to the left side.

·   Pay special attention to what happens when the finger crosses in front of the nose. Does the child lose focus? Do the eyes jump or wobble back and forth?

·   Place your finger near the end of the nose and ask the child to watch it as it moves.

·   Slowly pull the finger in and out from the nose.

·   Observe how the child's eyes work together. If they jump all over the place, it is time for a professional exam.

The eyes should move smoothly from one side of the body, across the midline and to the other side without difficulty and should remain focused on a finger close to the nose and when pulled farther away. Avoidance of the task suggests that the exercise is difficult or uncomfortable. Check with the classroom teacher to see how fluently the child reads or listen to him read at home. If reading is a problem, it may be time for a professional evaluation.

What to Do

A comprehensive vision examination should precede any form of intervention for vision problems. Such an exam should be conducted by a qualified professional, trained not only in prescribing lenses to achieve 20/20 vision, but also trained in identifying visual abnormalities.

If a problem is found, vision therapy may be recommended. Vision therapy, a type of physical therapy for the eyes and brain, is a highly effective, non-surgical treatment for many common visual problems such as lazy eye, crossed eyes, double vision, convergence insufficiency and some reading and learning disabilities. In the case of learning disabilities, vision therapy is specifically directed toward resolving visual problems that interfere with reading, learning and educational instruction. Vision therapy should not be considered a direct treatment for learning disabilities.

Vision therapy is a progressive program of vision exercises or procedures performed under a doctor's supervision. These procedures are individualized to fit the visual needs of each patient and are generally conducted in the doctor's office once or twice per week in sessions lasting 30 minutes to one hour. The objective is to help develop or improve fundamental visual skills and abilities or change how a patient processes or interprets visual information. Other objectives may include improving visual comfort, ease and efficiency.

Unlike some other forms of exercise, the goal of vision therapy is not to strengthen eye muscles; eye muscles are already incredibly strong! Vision therapy is not to be confused with any self-directed program of eye exercises marketed to the public. Vision therapy is supervised by optometric vision care professionals who use many types of specialized and/or medical equipment, such as:

- prescription lenses (regulated medical devices)
- therapeutic lenses (regulated medical devices)
- prisms (regulated medical devices)
- optical filters
- eye patches or occluders
- electronic targets with timing mechanisms
- computer software
- vestibular (balance) equipment

The first step in any vision therapy program is a comprehensive vision examination. Following a thorough evaluation, a qualified vision care professional can advise parents as to whether vision therapy would be an appropriate treatment. The School of Optometry at your local college or university would be a good place to begin if you are lucky enough to have one.

Interventions for Home and School

Given the numerous components of vision skills, one can imagine all the different ways in which visual processing difficulties might interfere with learning.

Below are some modifications and accommodations for successful intervention with your child's problem, both at home and in the classroom. It is recommended that the use of these strategies be matched with specific areas of weakness identified in a thorough vision examination.

It is important to understand that because vision is multifaceted, the same intervention does not work for everyone. Instructional strategies have to be developed to accommodate all the possible combinations of weaknesses within each individual child

There are two approaches used by schools to meet the needs of children with any kind of processing disorder. The first is to make changes in the physical space in the classroom (modifications) and the second is to make changes in teaching methods (accommodations).

This simply means that the teacher changes where the student is physically located within the classroom (modifications) and takes into consideration his learning style when teaching him (accommodations). The process of finding successful modifications and accommodations takes time and experimentation, but much time is saved if you work from the results of a through vision exam.

Visual perceptual processing can be broken into three components: visual spatial skills, visual analysis skills and visual integration skills. These skills coordinate almost simultaneously, and when one does not work well, all the others are affected. A child achieves best when everything is well integrated.[xlii]

Visual Spatial Skills[xliii]

These are the skills we use to understand and organize visual space. Visual spatial skills require observing an object, then accurately perceiving its relationship in space relative to our selves.

Laterality is the knowledge of right and left on one's own body. It is an internal self-awareness of two body sides and knowing they are different. It requires good balance, inner ear function and an awareness of body midline (an invisible line that divides your body in half top to bottom). Laterality eventually develops into directionality.

Directionality incorporates the concepts of up, down, ahead, behind and any combination of these. It also means projecting these directions, including left and right out into space. A person must understand these concepts as they relate to him before he can apply them to other things.

Maturation is the key to the development of this skill; significant improvement should be seen within the first year of school. Those who have continuing difficulty are considered to have a Developmental Coordination Disorder (DCD). This is a very complicated disorder; maturation and special training are the keys.

That is why specific diagnostic information is needed to design an appropriate educational program. The following signs and symptoms will help to determine if a problem exists. Accommodations are suggested for classroom and/or at home.

Signs and Symptoms

·   Has difficulty consistently perceiving the proper position of an object in relation to himself; may bump into things

·   May "miss" his seat when he sits down

·   May not understand the concepts of left, right, up, down, etc.

Accommodations

·   Rather than using the terms "left" and "right," use references such as "the side of the room with the windows" or "the side of the room with the door."

·   Indicate right and left by marking them on the student's desk.

·   Encourage more physical exercise, which will assist with overall neurological integration.

·   Have the child place one hand on his seat before sitting.

Visual Analysis Skills

Visual analysis or visual discrimination is comprised of seven different components. It is used to identify, sort, organize, store and recall information presented visually. It is the ability to take in visual information, remember it and apply it later.

Visual Figure-Ground Discrimination is the ability to locate a form or object within a busy field without getting confused by the background or surrounding images. This skill keeps children from getting lost in details. Children with poor figure-ground become easily confused with too much print on the page, which affects their concentration and attention. They may also have difficulty scanning text to locate specific information. A person with this difficulty will have difficulty finding a favorite object even when it is in plain sight.

Signs and symptoms

·   Difficulty finding a specific bit of information on a printed page full of words and numbers

·   Finding a same-colored pencil in a box of crayons

·   Finding a favorite book on a bookshelf

Accommodations

·   Put fewer problems on a page, with lots of space between each problem. In severe cases, present one problem at a time

·   Use larger print with a bolder font for reading and put less information on each page

·   Organize school supplies; separate pencils from crayons.

Visual Discrimination is the skill of using vision to distinguish one item from another based on its individual characteristics of color, form, shape, pattern, size, and position. A weakness in this area can make it difficult for one to learn to read, write and spell.

Signs and Symptoms

·   Confuses similarly shaped letters b/d, p/g, 3/E, p/q, on/no, 24/42.

·   Fails to accurately identify the difference between letters, numbers and symbols.

·   Has difficulty distinguishing between two similar letters, shapes or objects.

·   May not notice the similarities and differences between certain colors, shapes and patterns.

Accommodations

·   Eliminate competing shapes in instructional materials.

·   Anticipate confusion and point out examples of correct responses.

- Keep instructional materials simple and uncomplicated.
- Clearly space words or problems on a page.
- Consistently use the same font style in printed materials.

Visual closure is the ability to recognize a familiar object when only parts of it are visible.

Signs and Symptoms

- Has difficulty recognizing a truck without its wheels.
- Cannot identify a word with a letter missing.
- Has difficulty recognizing a face when one feature (such as the nose) is missing.

Accommodations

- Eliminate these challenges in instructional materials

Visual Form Constancy is the ability to recognize the same object when presented in different positions, or sizes.

Signs and Symptoms

- A word that is well known in one form, color, size, type of writing or in conjunction with certain other words may appear new to him/her when presented in another form, color, size, or context.

Accommodations

- Use same font, color, shape, and format in all instructional materials

Visual Speed is the speed with which one can locate, attend to, perceive and remember visual information when completing visual tasks. A person with this difficulty will take longer than normal with simple tasks.

Signs and Symptoms

- Does not complete work in allotted time.
- Is the last one to finish a visual task.
- Appears to be working hard but does not get anything done.

Accommodations

- Allow additional time for the completion of work.
- Grade him on the work that he does complete.

- Never make him finish during recess; he needs that time away from lessons even more than the others.
- Assign the amount of work that he will be able to complete in the time available (5 problems instead of 10).
- Allow the child to complete assignments at home.
- Give credit for the work completed.

Visual Memory is the ability to recall something seen some time ago (long-term) and the ability to remember something seen very recently (short-term).

Signs and Symptoms

- Has difficulty spelling familiar words with irregular spelling.
- Does not comprehend what he has read.
- Will not remember the alphabet when learned visually.
- Inaccuracy in reading and spelling sight words. .
- Does not recognize the same word used twice in a sentence.

Visual Sequential Memory is the ability to correctly recall the order of a series of letters or numbers like phone numbers or an address.

Signs and Symptom

- Cannot remember equations in mathematics.
- Does not recall phone numbers or addresses.
- Has difficulty copying accurately.

Accommodations

- Utilize a recorder and let him listen to information to be learned.
- Write down important information like phone numbers
- Have the child read instructions out loud so that he can hear them.
- Have him follow along as you read aloud.
- Use stronger auditory skills to teach phone numbers and addresses.
- Put books on tape and let him listen to a story.

Visual Integration

Ocular Motility refers to eye movement control. It is the ability to perform accurate and effective eye movement patterns. An individual with poor ocular motor control will have difficulty moving both eyes smoothly and accurately from word to word while reading and/or tracking moving objects. (See Sensori-Motor Skills).

Signs and Symptoms

- Turns head when reading across page or holds paper at odd angles.
- Often loses his place while reading.
- Repeats or omits words or lines of print while reading.
- Transposes letters or numbers while reading or copying.
- Fatigue and motion sickness
- Inaccurate eye-hand coordination.

Accommodations

- Use large-print books.
- Order or check out books on tape
- Use an index card with a rectangular window cut out to aid with tracking and to eliminate other distracting information on the page.
- For older children, use a straight-edge under the sentence to help keep the place while reading.
- Use a straight-edge made from colored construction paper for further contrast.
- Track the words by having the child point with a finger.

Binocularity is the ability to align both eyes accurately on an object and combine the visual images from each eye into a single perception with depth.

Signs and Symptoms

- Unstable vision, may see two objects or books
- Closes one eye while working; may yawn while reading
- Blurring of vision
- Light sensitivity
- Headache
- Dizziness
- Motion sickness
- Poor eye-hand coordination

·   Decreased concentration and distractibility.

Accommodations

·   If the child sees two books, have him focus on one and ignore the other or cover one eye while reading.

·   Seat him away from the bright light of the windows.

·   Let him put his head down and listen when fatigued.

·   Provide frequent breaks from any visual activity.

·   Put important information on tape and allow him to listen.

Accommodation

Accommodation (not the same as classroom accommodations) is the ability of the inside of the eye to reshape itself appropriately so that objects can be seen clearly at various distances.

Signs and Symptoms

·   Has difficulty refocusing from the board to the writing paper or from the teachers face to the book.

·   Cannot focus on objects at mid-range distance.

·   Has difficulty reading different size print on the same page.

Accommodations

·   Reduce visual stress by seating the child near the source of visual information, chalkboard or bulletin board.

·   Give the child permission to change his seat as needed for focus.

·   Leave his reading material where he places it to read.

Remember that classroom accommodations are designed to help the child to achieve. They are not a form of "treatment" or "intervention" to correct the problem.

Designing the Elementary School IEP

In elementary school, a child with visual processing problems may be described as getting poor grades because he does not complete assignments, fidgets, plays and interrupts the work of other students. Or he loses his place while reading because he is unable to follow a line of print across the page, confuses the sounds of letters, transposes numbers, does not write on

The IEP team must keep in mind that when the visual processing system is immature, engaging in visual tasks requires the expenditure of a great deal of energy. When this level of energy is expended during a visual task, the child experiences an early onset of fatigue before completing assignments and exhibits hyperactivity as the level of fatigue progresses. Because of the ensuing level of discomfort, the child avoids further visual activity, his attention wanders and he becomes a behavior problem. Five to 10 minutes is the maximum amount of time that a child with a visual processing disorder will be able to attend well at this level of development. The child should be monitored to determine the maximum amount of time that he can attend in a group and should be assigned activities that require that amount of time to complete.

Remember that the child is not lazy; requiring that he work beyond his capacity brings on a level of fatigue that creates a negative attitude toward all school work. Burn him out in the morning and imagine the terror he will be all afternoon. When fatigued to the point of hyperactivity, it takes up to 45 minutes of complete rest for the system to return to normal. The only remedy is not allowing the child to reach this level of fatigue. If you do allow the child to become over-fatigued, he will present as oppositional and defiant. Read this behavior as a warning signal to stop work and give him a rest break. Grade him on the work that he has completed. Ask for additional effort after he is rested.

Classroom Accommodations

The first consideration when planning accommodations is to identify areas of strength so that you can teach through those areas. If instructions are given visually, try to supplement this with auditory explanations. While it is important to strengthen areas of weakness, it should be remembered that learning is the primary objective.

Keep the area of difficulty in mind by using simple, uncomplicated visual information. Putting the information to be learned on tape, using fewer words and larger print per page and giving frequent breaks from visual activity can make a big difference to a person with visual processing difficulties.

Both teacher and parent can research and use specific activities that strengthen the areas of weakness. An excellent resource for these activities is www.ldinfo.com. Activities in the free manual are designed for self-directed students; however, the ideas can be readily adapted for home and classroom use.

Remember that classroom accommodations are designed to help the child to achieve. They are not a form of "treatment" or "intervention" to correct the problem. Correction of the problem is the responsibility of the parent, just as any other medical treatment would be.

There are many ways in which the child can be managed in the classroom:

· After each 5- to 10-minute period of maximum focus, provide a break that includes physical activity that requires him to get out of his seat and move around.

· Teach the child to monitor himself and give him permission to get out of his seat when he needs to. Download the above mentioned manual for him.

· Buy him a vibrating timer to remind him to get up and move around.

· Make the time out of his seat purposeful by assigning him to pass out papers and books. Let him maintain the book corner by rearranging and re-shelving books

· Have a social sharing where the rest of the class learns to respect the special needs of other children and the special accommodations in the classroom.

· Have him return some balls to the gym teacher. Pick up a ball each day and have him return it when he becomes fatigued from visual tasks. (Be sure to inform the gym teacher what you are doing).

· During recess, play a game that requires him to run, hop, skip, or jump (everyone will benefit from these activities because they help with sensori-motor integration).

· Grade him on the work that he is able to complete and move on to the next classroom activity.

· Never require him to return to his seat and complete his work unless he is rested sufficiently.

· Provide opportunity for the child to rest during the day. (One school principal kept a mat on the floor of her office where children were sent for a nap when they were fatigued.)

· Assign the same homework, but require completion of less work; i.e., complete 5 of the required 10 problems for homework (five correct problems demonstrates mastery as well as 10. Practice does not make perfect in the case of visual processing learning disabilities).

· The child should be taught to manage his fatigue with permission to get out of his seat and move about the room when he feels the aura of beginning fatigue.

· Shorten his school day. Schedule important things in the morning and let your learning disabled child leave school and finish his day at home. The travel time and being away from all the confusion of the classroom will perk him up and he will be ready to work again. If there is no one at home, the school library or resource teacher will do. These children state that the school day is just too long.

Accommodations at Home

· Never do homework right after school. After school should be a quiet time for rest and relaxation from the challenges to his nervous system during the school day. Read the chapter on sleep and have him take a nap. Three things will happen: his nervous system will relax, what he learned during the day will go into long-term memory and he will regenerate the energy needed to do his homework.

· Do homework after a rest period or just before going to bed. Work only for the length of time that he is able to attend. Never force him to complete the homework assignment by stretching homework into the midnight hours.

· Note how much reading or how many problems the child can do before he begins to slow down and stop working.

· Report this period of time, number of paragraphs or number of problems to the teacher and set his homework requirements accordingly. Have the teacher grade him on this amount of work.

· Provide a well-lighted, quiet place for him to study and play classical

(Baroque) music (research indicates it improves learning).

·   Monitor how well he does with and without your assistance and act accordingly.

Things to avoid

·   Assuming that the child is lazy because he will not complete the assignment.

·   Forcing him to work beyond the time when he is beginning to avoid the work.

·   Encouraging the child to do one more problem, accompanied by saying, "I know you can do better work than this."

·   Making him complete all the homework assignment "even if it takes all night," because it has, will and does take all night for a child with learning disabilities, whose nervous system has shut down with fatigue.

·   Criticism, anger and punishment for non-performance. Remember, the child has a learning disability; his brain is not doing what it should. What you see is the best he can give when fatigued. He will do better when he has rested. And, don't fail to be understanding, give him lots of love and acceptance (not encouragement to "Just try one more," and then when he does, another and another until he doesn't trust you anymore). Leave him alone, let him rest his system through physical exercise (go to the bathroom, get a drink of water, 12 to 20 minutes depending upon the level of fatigue) and then try one more.

What to Do

·   Get the child's eyes examined; be sure that he can see.

·   It may be that his eyes are not sufficiently matured to see the print in a third-grade text book. He may need to continue reading larger print for a while.

·   Find out by asking him which book he would prefer to read (show him large and small print, type the text in a larger font on your computer at home or enlarge it on a copy machine). Children are surprisingly insightful into what they are experiencing and often will make excellent recommendations for remedy. Don't try to figure it out by yourself. Ask the child what he is experiencing, then listen and try to work it out. Don't criticize what he is telling you. If you do, he won't tell you anything else and then you will be totally lost as to what to do.

·   When you learn these things, share them with the classroom teacher. If she doesn't listen, ask the school administrator for a team meeting. Advocate by talking with the principal. Ask for the school's 504 Plan. The 504 Plan is a description of how the school will accommodate the needs of children who do not need special education.

·   Assert yourself and you will be respected by the school; your child will be treated better if they like you. Never be aggressive and threaten the school. Horrible things will begin to happen to your child. The "squeaky wheel" gets the grease, but the non-threatening wheel gets greased more often and the love overflows to the child of the "squeaky wheel" that is also tactful and flattering.

Designing the Middle School IEP

A middle school student with visual processing difficulties may be described as not completing his work. He becomes a behavior problem the last half hour of class and spends a great deal of time at home on suspension from school. This student may get a good grade in physical education and science lab, but fails Social Studies, English and other courses where extensive reading is required.

The IEP team should keep in mind that in middle school, the 50-minute class period is much longer than the 30 minutes he is able to remain focused before becoming hyperactive and a behavior problem. Depending upon the level of maturation, the amount of time he is able to spend on visual tasks may vary according to the developmental level of his visual system. Ask for the age equivalent of your child's visual processing abilities. The response should read: "Performs at a level comparable to the average child of age 8 or 10 (or some other age)."

The child's age equivalent will give you a clue about where to begin. An age equivalent of 8 is interpreted as being comparable to the visual skills of an 8-year-old child. Therefore, his middle school work should be presented with materials comparable to those used with 8-year-olds. This means larger print, fewer words per page, fewer problems to be done as homework and smaller written assignments, but with middle school concepts and ideas. Don't water down the curriculum content; modify the way in which the information is presented.

Classroom Accommodations/Modifications

· Note the period of time that he can stay focused and provide hands-on projects, research in the back of the room and individual problem-solving activity to be completed while he is on break from visual tasks.

· Make him the hall monitor and arrange for him to take the roll to the office at the end of 30 minutes. The gross motor activity of physically moving around will stabilize his nervous system and he will attend the last 15 minutes of class. This will save the child from detention and suspension for problem behavior.

· Seat him in the front of the room so that when he is off-task, there is no one in front of or around him to disturb. This also reduces distractions and the teacher can keep a better eye on him.

· Monitor the child to determine his maximum attention span, then build in activities for him to do that do not require the level of visual focus needed for reading.

· Shorten his school day. Home-school the child for two hours at the end of the day, followed by a nap. He will do it if you insist; set limits.

· Schedule his major subjects in the morning before he gets tired.

· Nothing major after lunch; he is burned-out and sleepy.

· Monitor his diet: no sugar, white flour or soft drinks.

· Teach the child to monitor himself. Have a social studies lesson to teach the other children to appreciate the "special needs" of their classmates so they don't expect the same "privileges."

· Make arrangements for the child to report to the counselor's office when all else fails. Be sure to inform the counselor of what you are doing and write it into the IEP or a 504 Plan for the child.

Modifications and Accommodations at Home

· Talk with the child about what he is experiencing.

· Communicate to the child that you understand his challenges as he describes them.

· Listen when he expresses his frustrations.

·   Help him to put his feelings into words; suggest the name of feelings.

·   Always remain positive.

·   Stop working with him when you feel yourself becoming frustrated.

·   Accept that he is tired when he says he is and say "we'll work some more later."

·   Get the teacher to accept the amount of homework that he is able to do.

·   Have fun with him; treat him as if you value him and think he is worthwhile.

Things to Avoid

·   Criticizing the child and telling him to act his age, because that is what he is doing—acting his age equivalent, at least. And remember, his visual nervous system is not mature and not under voluntary control; he is doing the best he can.

·   Making the assumption that the child is lazy; making statements like, "I know you can do better work than this." He can do better work when he is not fatigued out of his mind and has lost control of his senses. Never punish the child for this behavior. Give him a rest break and he will do good work again.

·   Punishing the child for unsatisfactory behavior without making the proper modifications to accommodate his "special needs."

·   Assuming that the child cannot learn or that he has poor cognitive ability. Being identified as learning disabled requires that you have at least average intelligence. The child is tired, fatigued and exhausted but not retarded.

A note to the academician: Conceptualization as a learning disability has been witnessed by this author as a phenomenon that occurs when challenges from visual processing have exhausted the student to a point of dysfunction in all areas. Therefore, conceptualization—the inability to formulate rational ideas for problem-solving—is not treated as a separate learning disability but is rather addressed here by the suggestion that the child will again be able to conceptualize appropriately when rested from his exhaustion.

A note to teachers and parents: Do not engage these children physically when they are exhausted from fatigue or have become oppositional. One child stated that the teacher did not understand and that she kept pushing him to do more, even when he stated that he was too tired. When she physically redirected the child to his work, the 75-pound boy lost control and the 175-pound teacher spent three days in the hospital and did not return to work for some time. Respect the child and the child will respect you.

What to Do

If he has made it to middle school without improvement, it is because proper accommodations were not implemented earlier. (Read the interventions above, under elementary school and choose those that will work).

· Get his eyes examined and try something like visual training at the local college or university.

· Talk with a good optometrist who examines for more than the need for glasses. Good optometrists are out there and some of them do really fantastic visual training. Look under visual training on the Internet and check out a local kinesiologist. These professionals are expensive; if you are working two jobs to make ends meet, it is not likely that you will want to make a major financial investment. In that case, a 504 Plan is appropriate. Request that the school do an evaluation and find out what accommodations are needed.

· Get mad about all the disciplinary suspensions. Your child is not learning while he is sitting at home on suspension. Ask the school to find out why his behavior is acceptable in gym and science and not in social studies. There is something different about the expectations and/or environment in the classes and your child's ability to conform in different settings. It is the school's responsibility to find out these things. It is your responsibility to see that they do what they are responsible for doing.

Designing an Appropriate High School IEP

A high school student who is not receiving an appropriate

education may be described as: avoids all work, cuts class, is truant and dropped out to go to work or just loaf around.

School is the only place where the student does not feel worthwhile. He has average intelligence and he knows that what he is being taught is not relevant to real life. If he has not learned to read well by now and the school continues to give him the same old reading lessons, he is made to feel that he is not worth the effort of trying to teach him what he is able to learn. This blow to his self-esteem makes him angry and defensive. School becomes a very painful place and he avoids going there except to see his friends.

High school students with learning disabilities have been made painfully aware that they have a learning problem and that they are different. By now, they have been segregated into special classes, in which they come into contact only with other students with similar learning problems. They are left out of extra-curricular activities except for sports, where they are exploited by playing hard and not accepted by the rest of the team. The captain of the football team is never the special class LD student. The prom king is seldom the special education student. The learning disabled are second-class students at their school and they deserve to be integrated into the mainstream of the student body.

It is only in the out-of-school environment that they feel worthwhile; it has been demonstrated over and over that learning disabilities are evident only at school. Out of school, they look just like everyone else and if they have had the opportunity to learn them, they have good social skills.

You will have to advocate for your child to see that he learns what he is capable of learning and that his IEP or 504 Plan reflects an emphasis in the areas where he is outstanding and can excel. If he is good in math and fails social studies, let him study more math applications. If math is difficult, find out what he does learn well and let him study that. Do not sit still as your child learns nothing because he is learning disabled. Remember, he still has average intelligence and evidently has learned something or he would not remain in the average range of ability.

Unfortunately, if he is not receiving an appropriate education, he will eventually test below average. Remember that these children can learn; we just have to identify the modalities through which they learn best. That is the responsibility of the school. The child's most effective learning modality should have been identified early and utilized through the grades.

Classroom Accommodations/Modifications

This is the simplest yet the most challenging of all levels to accommodate. It is simple to say "make learning relevant," but it is another matter to remain true to the state curriculum guidelines. At any rate, the school has the responsibility to provide an "appropriate" education for your child.

- Talk with the child and find out what he would like to be learning and then teach it to him (with some reservations, of course).
- If he can't read, read the book into a recorder and let him listen to it.
- Read the book to him while he answers the questions in the homework assignment.
- Read the contents of the lesson aloud and then discuss it with the student.
- Allow oral responses to tests. Examination is for the purpose of finding out what a child knows. He should not be penalized because of his poor handwriting skills.
- Let the student develop his own curriculum by doing some teacher-pupil planning at the end of each grading period.
- Evaluate what the student has learned so far and make plans for the next grading period.
- Create rap music with positive lyrics. Make a rap about the social studies lesson.
- Instead of literature, read something relevant like a computer manual or a repair manual for his car. Read it, teach it and have him respond.
- Social studies should be about employment, being a good citizen, finding a job, the kinds of work people do and the kinds of manufacturing concerns in the area that employ local people. Would the student like to work there and why? What is an employee and what makes a good one?

Things to Avoid

·   Avoid teaching materials with content relevant to a younger student. The learning-disabled student is immature only in the area of his specific learning disability; emotionally and psychologically he is a teenager. Simply teach him what he is interested in. To find out what that is, you must ask him. The material can be modified in order to fit within the boundaries of the state curriculum guidelines.

·   Avoid the negative effects of your comments upon the student's self-esteem. You will earn his respect by respecting him as an adult with a desire to succeed. Regardless of how he behaves or the comments he throws back over his shoulder, he wants to be successful.

·   Avoid a boring learning environment with bare walls and bulletin board and a boring teacher dressed like a bum. As a teacher, the best way to respect your students is to dress nicely but casually. Students do not respect a teacher who looks like a peer. Look like a peer, and you will be treated as a peer.

What to Do

·   Don't allow your student to remain distant from you, alone in his own world, with parents who are uninvolved and uncaring. Get involved, talk with him and listen. If he won't let you help with homework, take an active interest. Assist with research; get involved with the science project.

·   Build a relationship with your child, such that your attention is sufficient reward for working harder at achieving in school. (No, I'm not dreaming. In high school this author's one goal in life was to please her parents. That changed some time later.)

·   Listen when your child talks and he will tell you everything. Then, when you talk with the school about IEPs and 504 Plans, it will be like advocating for your alter ego. In conferences, you will be talking about him as a person whom you know better than the teacher who sees him only 55 minutes per day.

·   Find out from your child what school feels like, what he likes and dislikes and what he thinks he should be learning.

·   Evaluate it and then communicate it to the school administrator and teacher.

·   Check with your child to see if he likes his new class any better and if not, make another phone call. Let the school know that it would be best for all concerned if you don't have to "make another a trip up to that school." Remember to be tactful.

·	Many high school students have physical disabilities that have never been diagnosed and treated. Get a vision exam; check his diet and his health. Has he been injured playing football or soccer? Does he have headaches? Is his neck sore?

·	At the annual re-evaluation, ask that the school psychologist evaluate your child to identify his most effective learning modality (does he learn best what he hears or what he sees?) Again, these should have been identified in the early grades and utilized throughout the years.

·	When visual processing is a problem, develop an IEP or 504 Plan that emphasizes auditory learning. (If he has to "read" a novel, get it on tape at the public library and have him listen to it or read it into a tape recorder yourself).

·	Make books on tape part of his IEP 504 Plan. Let the school worry about how they are going to get the books onto the tape. There are lots of students around who would appreciate the opportunity to do the job. Don't use a friend or anyone whom he knows. Let the voice be an unfamiliar one unless he has a trusted friend whose voice will be welcome.

Visual processing deficits sometimes include poor visual memory. That is, a child cannot remember what he has just read and five minutes later may not remember what he has just been exposed to visually. If he is not reading in high school, it may be due to poor visual memory. Your 504 Plan should reflect his need for a program similar to that of visually impaired children. Not remembering it is similar to not seeing it; either way, it does not get into long-term memory. Insist upon the same consideration for your child with poor visual memory as for other children with severe visual handicaps.

The visual mechanism develops slowly. Ask for a complete initial evaluation to determine your child's strengths and weaknesses. The law states that he has to be re-evaluated every three years. Insist that this re-evaluation be more than to determine if a discrepancy still exists so that he can stay in special education. For many children it has been years since they have received a complete evaluation to determine their learning needs. You should get one, and rewrite the IEP or 504 Plan. So what if he hasn't changed any.

At least you will know that he should begin receiving some vocational education and preparation for gainful employment.

Insist upon the development of employable skills. The law says that your child's education should be appropriate and it is appropriate for a child to be prepared for employment if he is not going to college.

CHAPTER XV

AUDITORY PROCESSING

Auditory processing is the term used to describe what happens when your brain recognizes and interprets the sounds around you. Humans hear when sound waves travel through the ear and are changed into electrical information that can be interpreted by the brain. A child is considered to have a deficit in this area when there is evidence that something is adversely affecting the processing or interpretation of the information. The problem is not with how well the child hears information, but rather with how the auditory nervous system processes and interprets the information that is heard.

Central Auditory Processing Disorder, diagnosed by professionals such as speech and language therapists and/or audiologists, is not the same disorder that is identified by the school psychologist. A child with Central Auditory Processing is eligible for special education services but is not identified as having a learning disability.

An auditory processing deficit identified by the school psychologist and considered to be a learning disability is much less severe, is identified using less specific tests and presents with far milder symptoms. If the school psychologist finds that the processing problem seems severe, the child will be referred to the speech and language therapist who, after determining a need for further evaluation, will make a referral to an audiologist.

However, even mild weakness in auditory processing as identified by the school psychologist can affect how a child acquires language skills, learns in school (particularly reading) and can impact educational and social communication skills. The more profound the symptoms, the greater the potential they have to interfere with academic achievement.

Symptoms of Possible Auditory Processing Difficulty[xlvi]

Children with auditory processing difficulty typically have normal hearing and intelligence. Behaviorally, they may:

·   Have trouble paying attention to and remembering information presented orally
·   Have problems carrying out multi-step directions
·   Have poor listening skills
·   Need more time to process information
·   Have low academic performance
·   Have behavior problems
·   Have language difficulty (e.g., they confuse syllable sequences and have problems developing vocabulary and understanding language)
·   Have difficulty with reading, comprehension, spelling, and vocabulary

How Does This Happen

Auditory processing disorders may be genetic and have a tendency to occur in families or the child may have been exposed to some trauma during gestation. Auditory processing disorders may also be present as a result of immature development. In some instances it may also relate to a lack of auditory experiences.

The listening skills of children who are not adequately exposed to all of the speech sounds and listening experiences that are typically encountered by young infants and young children may not be fully developed. Considerable data suggests that children who experience frequent middle ear infections during critical auditory development periods (such as the first and second years of life) fall in this category.

Overall, the ability to recognize and separate sounds in the environment requires training via learning experiences. No matter the reason (ear infection, brain injury, genetic factor, etc.), if there is a time during critical developmental stages when the auditory stimuli does not or cannot ger in, the brain cells that normally process hearing do not learn how to do so. The result is a deficit in the brain's ability to process auditory information.

Educational Implications

When instruction in school relies primarily on spoken language, the child with an auditory processing weakness may have varying degrees of difficulty understanding the lesson or the directions. There are several types of auditory processing disorders, each affecting different aspects of auditory information processing and having a unique impact upon learning. A child with an auditory processing deficit may experience a weakness in one or several of the following aspects of auditory processing.

Aspects of Auditory Information Processing[xlv]

Phonological awareness is the ability to hear that language is made up of individual sounds (phonemes) that are put together to form the words we write and speak. This is an important precursor to reading, writing and understanding spoken language.

Signs and Symptoms

· Does not recognize similarities between words (as in rhyming words)

· Does not hear phonemes

· Fails to isolate individual sounds in words

· Cannot break a word into its component sounds

Accommodations

· If visual memory is intact, emphasize sight reading for all words.

Auditory discrimination is the ability to recognize differences between sounds or words that are similar. This problem can affect following directions, reading, spelling and writing skills.

Signs and Symptoms

- Misinterprets comments in social situations
- Does not do well in group work
- Cannot write from dictation
- Misspells common words
- May spell the same word differently in the same sentence

Accommodations

- Grade only in areas of strength, do not penalize in this area
- Modify instruction that requires this skill for comprehension

Auditory Memory is the ability to store or retain pertinent information that one hears for use now (short-term) or later (long-term). It may affect ability to follow oral directions, participate in discussion and spell.

Signs and Symptoms

- Has difficulty following two-step directions
- Does not maintain correct sequence of letters in spelling
- Does not attend in group settings
- Has difficulty spelling unfamiliar words

Accommodations

- Write down two or three main points for him to listen for and check for memory and understanding of those points.
- Break complicated directions into fewer parts and allow time to complete the first step before going on to the second.

Auditory figure-ground discrimination is the ability to understand spoken language in a noisy background; and may show up more in noisy environments or when expected to listen for information.

Signs and Symptoms

- Does not respond when the TV is on
- Cannot distinguish the teacher's voice over the noise in the classroom

Accommodations

- Seat him away from visual and auditory distractions such as fans, heaters, windows, doors, pencil sharpeners.
- Allow him to move to a quiet area or wear earplugs when doing silent reading and independent work
- Enforce good communication rules: one person talks at a time; others listen quietly
- Use simple, expressive sentences
- Speak at a slightly slower rate and at a mildly increased volume

Auditory sequencing is remembering the order of spoken words or sounds in a series.

Signs and Symptoms

- Does not remember phone numbers or addresses
- Has difficulty memorizing auditory information
  Accommodations

- Use his strengths to convey information—write it down
- Accompany verbal instruction with written or visual cues

Auditory blending is combining isolated sounds to form words.

Signs and Symptoms

- Has difficulty blending sounds into words
- Has poor word attack skills
- Cannot decipher compound words
  Accommodations

- Use his stronger visual skills, teach sight reading.
- Rhyming games can help build phonological awareness.
- Avoid using this skill in evaluations; use oral tests.
- Do not penalize child for mistakes in this area.

Auditory Attention is the ability to maintain focus for listening.
Signs and Symptoms

- Cannot maintain attention to the teacher's voice
- Does not maintain focus long enough to hear instructions

Accommodations

- Gain his attention before giving new work or directions
- Speak clearly with a moderate rate and stand in one place, facing him; have him look at you when receiving instructions

Auditory Cohesion is when higher-level listening tasks are difficult.

Signs and Symptoms

- Cannot draw inferences from conversation, understand riddles or comprehend verbal math problems
- Doesn't understand puns and jokes, often becomes a social isolate

Accommodations

- Allow him a longer time to respond—beyond what you might consider normal when asking questions.
- Simplify/explain new vocabulary; encourage him to ask questions for clarification
- Give concrete interesting examples, demonstrations and written or pictorial information when presenting new concepts

What to Do

If your child has been identified as having an auditory problem and he is in second or third grade, it is likely that he is simply immature in this area. Some of the skills a child needs in order to be evaluated for central auditory processing disorder don't develop until the age of eight or nine years.

The auditory center of the brain isn't fully developed at seven, eight and nine, the most common ages at which children are referred for the central auditory processing test. If your child falls within this age range, it is likely that with maturation he will develop these skills later. However, it is always best to get a professional evaluation to determine the exact nature of your child's problem.

Additionally, if your child has a central auditory processing deficit, you probably noticed it long before he went to school. Auditory processing problems range from mild to severe. If it was identified by the school psychologist and referred to as an auditory processing deficit, it is probably a milder condition and simple modifications should help until he matures in this area. If learning does not improve with simple classroom modifications, then the problem is more serious.

Caution!!

When a person has a disability, the impact on the family can be even more devastating than on the person's academics or work. Coping with and compensating for processing deficits at school or work can be exhausting, yet many people are far more successful at dealing with their difficulties in a structured work or school environment or in public than they are at home.

At home, no one wants to work that hard. Home is a place for putting your feet up, letting your hair down and being yourself. Frustrations that were suppressed at school or work may be transferred to family members at home. Sheer exhaustion may make for a grumpy, tearful child; a sullen, withdrawn teenager or an angry adult. Many of us have these tendencies after a hard day at work or school, but they may be much more pronounced in the person with an auditory processing deficit.

A large percentage of families with a handicapped child wind up divorced. Your handicapped child needs your advocacy and support, but so does the rest of the family. Don't become a statistic. You and your child need an intact family now more than ever. Imagine what it will be like for the child if he has the additional burden of being "split" in joint custody and has to spend weekdays here, weekends there or summers across the country trying to adapt to two different environments and having difficulty understanding what is expected of him.

Imagine the scolding and punishment from people who do not understand the nature of his difficulty even though he is giving 100 percent of what he has to give. Imagine how much of your time it will take for you to educate everyone in the new environments that he may experience.

Instead of taking time away from your family in order to advocate for your handicapped child, learn to manage your time and set some priorities. This is not the time to accept the position you have been eyeing on the board of that prestigious non-profit. You may have to give up your girl's night out, the presidency of your bridge club or drop out all together. It will be a constant battle of deciding what is important to you, setting priorities and managing time.

Designing an Appropriate

Individualized Education Plan

In children, auditory processing problems may be identified by speech and language problems, sensitivity to sounds, poor attention, difficulty following directions, difficulty expressing oneself, difficulty with listening and reading comprehension and difficulty with social interactions or auditory self-stimulation, such as constant humming or self-talk.

The IEP team should keep in mind that auditory processing problems differ from problems involving hearing, such as deafness or being hard of hearing. The child has a very real problem with interpreting what he hears and he has no control over it. He may be giving you 100 percent of what he has to offer and needs your support, understanding and involvement.

Much research still is needed to understand auditory processing problems and related disorders, as well as the best intervention for each child. Several strategies are available to help children with auditory processing difficulties; some of them are available commercially but have not been fully studied. The effectiveness of any strategy should first be evaluated and then used only with the guidance of a team of professionals. The speech and language therapist at your school is a good place to start.

Appropriate classroom behavior depends upon the ability to make sense from the environment, make decisions, take appropriate action and achieve academically. It is all a reflection of auditory processing. Academically, a child with auditory processing problems will struggle, unable to keep up with his age mates; a large percentage will drop out of school as soon as possible. These consequences make it necessary to write an Individualized Education Plan. The many ways in which an auditory deficit might occur make it imperative that the specific nature of your child's problem be identified in order to make the plan appropriate.

Classroom Accommodations[xlv]

Accommodations should be aimed at the specific needs of the child. No two children share the same set of strengths or areas of weakness. An effective intervention is one that utilizes a child's strengths in order to build on the specific areas needing development. Therefore, interventions should be viewed as a dynamic and ever-changing process. Although this may sound over-whelming initially, it is important to remember that the process of finding successful interventions becomes easier with time and as the child's learning approach, style and abilities are more clearly defined.

Children diagnosed with a full-blown Central Auditory Processing Disorder are sometimes accommodated in the general education classroom, so let's look at some ways in which your child with an auditory processing learning disability can be accommodated in the general education classroom also. Below are some general modifications that can accommodate your child at home and in the classroom. Remember that the process of finding successful accommodations takes time and experimentation.

The first consideration when planning interventions and accommodations is to teach to an area of strength. If instructions are given orally, try to supplement this with written or other visual cues. While it is important to address the area of need directly and try to build up areas of weakness, it is also necessary that the student progress on schedule with achievement.

The second consideration is to keep the area of difficulty in mind. Simplifying verbal directions, slowing the rate of speech and minimizing distractions can make a big difference to a person with auditory processing difficulties.

Next, it helps to plan specific activities for the areas of difficulty. There are many activities that can help build auditory processing skills, whether in the area of phonological awareness, auditory discrimination or any of the other deficits in this area. Rhyming games and discriminating between similar and different sounds can help build phonological awareness. Sorting games can help build auditory memory.

To more closely identify your child's specific weakness, observe carefully and utilize the signs, symptoms and recommended accommodations listed below.

Here are some modifications to the classroom environment that should prove helpful for auditory processing problems.

Seating

·   Select seating for the child away from auditory and visual distractions, in order to help maintain focus and attention.

·   A seat close to the teacher and the blackboard, away from the window and the door, may be helpful.

·   If the quiet area is near a window or door, seat the child with his back toward the distracting stimulus.

To Improve the Listening Environment

·   Give the child personal instruction by touching him on the shoulder and speaking directly to him when finished giving instructions to the class as a whole.

·   Identify the specific problem academic areas and provide whatever aids may help in class, such as an assignment pad or a tape recorder.

·   Reduce background noise. Find a quiet place to work.

·   Reduce external visual and auditory distractions. A large display of posters or cluttered bulletin boards can be distracting.

·   A study carrel in the room may help.

·   Ear plugs may be useful for reducing the distracting noise from a heater or air conditioner, pencil sharpener or talking in the hallway. Check with an audiologist to find out if ear plugs are appropriate and which kind to use. Placing mats and cloth poster boards on classroom walls has been shown to decrease the noise level.

·   A structured classroom setting in which students move around less frequently may be more beneficial than an open classroom situation.

When Talking to the Child with[xlvii]

Auditory Processing Deficits

· Speak slowly and clearly but do not exaggerate speech.

· Use simple, brief directions.

· Give directions in a logical, time-oriented sequence. Use words that make the sequence clear, such as first, next, finally.

· Use visual aids and write instructions to supplement spoken information.

· Emphasize key words when speaking or writing, especially when presenting new information.

· Pre-instruction with emphasis on the main ideas may be effective.

· Vary loudness to increase attention.

· Check comprehension by asking the child questions or asking for a brief summary after key ideas have been presented to be sure he understands.

· Paraphrase instructions and information in shorter and simpler sentences rather than by repeating.

· Encourage the child to ask questions for further clarification.

· Make instructional transitions clear.

· Review previously learned material.

· Recognize periods of fatigue and give breaks as necessary.

· Avoid showing frustration when the child misunderstands a message

· Avoid asking the child to listen and write at the same time.

· Give personal instruction by touching the child on the shoulder and speaking directly to the chil when finished giving group instructions.

At Home

- Have the child look at you when you are speaking.
- Use simple, uncomplicated sentences.
- Speak at a slightly slower rate and at a mildly increased volume.

· Ask the child to repeat the directions back to you ("What did you hear me say?" or "What are you going to do?") and tell him to continue to repeat them aloud (to himself) until the directions are completed.

- Provide a quiet place for your child to study.
- Organize a routine and do things on a regular time schedule.

·   Reduce background noise by turning the TV or radio off when no one is watching or listening. (You might enjoy the peace and quiet, also).

- See that the child gets plenty of rest. He works harder at hearing than you or other children.
- When he isolates himself, let him be away from the noise for awhile; put him to bed on time.

·   Pamper yourself; relax in a bubble bath after everyone else is asleep. You are the glue that holds this thing together. Be prepared, reward yourself.

Things to Avoid

·   Never punish the child for not following instructions (the most important thing you can do is to realize that auditory processing difficulties are real. Symptoms and behaviors are not within the child's control).

·   Try not to become frustrated with the child.

·   Provide structure and a time for routine activity.

·   The child can use the cues from routine activity to know what to do next.

CHAPTER XVI

SENSORI-MOTOR INTEGRATION

The term motor relates to muscle activity and the resulting body movements. Sensori-motor refers to the way in which the senses interact with the muscles to make the body move.

Other terms are often used to refer to this same process. Many terms refer to the specific nature of the problem, the muscles involved, and the severity of the disability. These skills are also referred to as developmental apraxia (muscular immaturity), graphomotor dyscoordination (poor handwriting), visual-perceptual-motor dysfunction (visual-motor with how we interpret the world around us) and non-verbal learning disabilities (a global term covering all the above, along with a few others).

Regardless of the complicated name, they all refer in some way to how the brain communicates with the muscles in the body and how well these two systems integrate within the individual child.[xxiv]

In the classroom, a lack of communication between the senses and the muscles is most commonly seen as immaturity in the use of the small muscles of the hands and fingers, referred to as fine motor control, and may show up as poor handwriting. When it is in the larger muscles of the body, it is referred to as gross motor control. A weakness in this area results in a clumsy child who appears to trip over his own feet and may be poor at sports. The other commonly recognized area of sensori-motor difficulty is referred to as visual-motor, which results in poor reading skills.

Each of these skills is examined in depth to assist with identifying needed modifications and accommodations for the development of an IEP, as well as for possible interventions at home.

Fine Motor Coordination

At one time, we could safely say that we did not know why the muscles, eyes, hand and brain sometimes do not communicate well. However, with advances in technology, scientists are looking into the brain and making new discoveries regarding growth and development.

Assuming the absence of other forms of environmental trauma, research suggests a relationship between under-developed sensori-motor skills and children spending hours sitting still in front of the television, passively entertained by playing video games, or interacting with a computer. These activities have cut sharply into the gross motor physical activities normal to childhood such as baseball, running, hopping, skipping, climbing trees or playing jacks. These are the activities that assist in developing the well-integrated sensory motor communication needed for reading, writing and learning.

Another factor is that shortly before the advent of TV and computers, schools stopped teaching handwriting. Remember the Palmer method of handwriting? As a child you might have filled a page with loops and ovals, sticks, teepees, push-pulls, running ovals, loop-de-loops and other patterns. This practice went on for weeks before you were taught how to form letters and it continued for years after. Well, there was method in that madness. All those running ovals and loop-de-loops were designed to train fine muscles and make the necessary neural connections in the central nervous system before attempting the more advanced skill of forming letters and making words.

Neuroscientists are bolstering this argument with new insights into the link between hand and brain. Research reveals that nothing can begin to compare with the neurological impact that rhythmic, repetitive manipulation of the thumb and fingers has in stabilizing the young brain.

One hundred years ago, Maria Montessori advocated the fundamental need to teach handwriting before reading. She gained worldwide fame for teaching Rome's "mentally retarded" street urchins how to read by the time they were five or six years old. Extensive brain research now validates her position. The phenomenon lies in the fact that the brain receives extensive physiological stimulation during the handwriting process, which helps ready the left brain for reading. As an interactive sensory process, training in handwriting ensures further brain growth, which increases its capacity for language development and language-based learning.[xxv]

Signs and Symptoms of Need for Training in Handwriting[xxvi]

Spatial Ordering Problem: (Decreased awareness regarding the spatial arrangement of letters, words, or sentences on a page).

- Poor use of lines on the paper
- Organizational problems
- Uneven spacing between letters
- Many misspelled words

Sequential Ordering Problem: (Difficulty putting letters, processes or ideas in order).

- Poor letter formation
- Transposed letters and spelling omissions

- Poor narrative sequencing
- Lack of transitions

Graphomotor Problem: (Inability to coordinate the small muscles of the fingers in order to maneuver a pen or pencil, especially as assignment length increases).

- Writes only very short passages
- Writes exceptionally slowly and with great effort
- Uses an awkward pencil grip
- Lacks fluidity in cursive writing
- Finds it hard to form letters
- Sloppy writing or drawing skills
- Can't stay on or in the lines
- Erases excessively
- Does not recognize mistakes
- Poor posture when writing
- Excessive or inadequate pencil grip
- Trouble aligning numbers in columns for math problems
- Can't get answers on paper
- Tests poorly on written tests even if the student knows the subject
- Poor coordination in sports
- Low self-esteem
- Unwillingness to try new challenges
- Avoidance behaviors when required to write

Classroom Accommodations

- Provide training in handwriting.
- Have daily activity using modeling clay.
- Written assignments should be shorter and written work should not be graded.
- Student should be able to give oral responses to any form of evaluation of knowledge learned.
- Tape recordings should substitute for written assignments.

·   A keyboard or computer should substitute in difficult cases.

·   Provide additional time for written assignments.

·   Grade content of written work, not the writing.

·   Modify or eliminate timed assignments.

·   Use graph paper to keep place value in math, or to space letters in writing.

·   Teach the student to play jacks or pick-up sticks. If you can't find jacks, use stones and a golf ball.

Accommodations at Home

Systematic handwriting instruction can and should be provided in every district, school and classroom, because all children deserve the benefits that accompany legible handwriting. And while it is true that students who are taught to write legibly have an advantage in daily writing, on standardized tests and in life, this need not be the fate of your child, because even adults can develop their skill in handwriting.[xxvii] For your child, handwriting can be developed at home as part of a recreational activity using therapeutic music that can be shared by the whole family.

The power of therapeutic music is well established. It affects heart rate, blood pressure and the nervous system.[xxviii] Exercising cortical neurons by listening to classical, Baroque-type music (Mozart) with 60-80 beats per minute (not rap, rock-n-roll or jazz) calms the brain and strengthens circuits used for mathematics. Plato once said that music is a more potent instrument than any other for education. Now scientists know why. Music, they believe, trains the brain for higher forms of thinking.[xxix] "Music helps to create a peaceful, relaxed environment, prime for learning and using long-term memory."[xxx]

Movement and therapeutic music *"retrains the brain"* and unlocks a child's potential. This means that if your child's handwriting, along with yours, is not what you would like it to be, you and your child can put on some classical music and have fun practicing loops, circles and slanted lines, loop-de-loops, teepees and push-pulls together. Fill pages with them until they become orderly and perfectly formed. Begin with lined paper, and then advance to unlined paper.

Visual Motor Integration[xxxi]

Visual motor integration is the ability to smoothly coordinate the movement of the eyes with each other and other parts of the body. Head, neck and eyes must move in a smooth, coordinated manner in order for the child to read well. If they do not, the child will often lose his place while reading or read the same sentence twice. The flow of reading is often jerky and the child will turn his whole head, using his neck to compensate for the lack of movement of the eyes.

Eye and Hand Coordination consists of coordinating visual skills with gross and fine-motor movement. It is the ability to integrate visual input with motor output. It is essential in academic performance. A practical application of this is the ability to copy from the board or from one page to another. This is the area that provides a diagnostic clue that a problem with sensori- integration may exist.

Eye and Body Movement refers to the fact that how our body moves in space is directed by our eyes. A visual motor problem may be suspected in the individual who frequently bumps into things when walking or a child who, when sitting down, may "miss" the chair and fall on the floor.

Visual-motor integration is achieved developmentally with maturation of the physical body. An infant may have eyes that just do not move well together and will tend to jerk back to the starting position when they are moved to the right or left. This behavior is normal in an infant; the eyes do not mature sufficiently for fluent reading until the child is five years old. This is the factor that sets the entry age for kindergarten.

However, with developmental immaturity, an older child may continue to have difficulty following a moving object for even a short distance before the eyes will jerk back to an earlier position. In some instances, the eyes may move smoothly to the midline of the body (the imaginary line that divides the body into right and left sides), where they will appear to jerk, causing a loss of focus on the object.

With jerking at the midline of the body, the opposite eye will pick up the object and follow it through to that side of the body. If this happens when an older child is reading, the words may appear to jump around on the page and the child will lose his place in the middle of a page if the book is in front of him. Children often learn to place the book on the right or left side of their midline to eliminate this problem. For some children there is a blind spot at the midline. The width of the blind spot will depend upon the severity of the problem. (See test at the end of Chapter I. This activity may also be used to train the eyes).

Children who cannot cross the midline of their body with their eyes may also exhibit difficulty crossing their midline with their hands. When standing at the blackboard, they will transfer the pencil or piece of chalk to the other hand when they reach the midline of their body and continue drawing the remainder of the line with the other hand. This is known as a lack of bi-lateral integration.

Bi-Lateral Integration is the ability to use both sides of the body simultaneously (like typing or riding a bicycle).

Signs and Symptoms

- Cannot visually track an object across the midline of the body.
- Switches hands so that one hand does not cross the midline of the body.
- Rotates the body so that he does not have to cross the midline.
- Does not use the non-dominant hand to support the paper when writing or drawing.
- Loses his place when reading.
- Can read words in isolation but cannot read them in a sentence.
- Avoids all reading tasks; does not read for pleasure.
- Has poor reading comprehension.

Accommodations

- Allow the child to place his writing paper or reading material in any position that he finds comfortable.
- Allow the child to position his body where he finds it most comfortable for reading.
- Encourage more physical activity to assist with physical development.
- Use a straight-edge above sentences to prevent the child from losing his place while reading. (The author learned to place the straight-edge

under sentences, but learned recently that the eyes move up when focusing, so placing the straight-edge above the line makes it easier to keep one's place.)

·   Protect the child's ego by not requiring him to read aloud in the presence of other students.

·   Use larger print with bolder font.

Praxis

Praxis is the process of getting the idea, initiating, planning and completing new motor tasks (muscle movements). It is the end product of input and integration of information from the sense of touch, balance and movement, the inner ear, vision and hearing, all of which may be necessary for good execution of motor activities. There are several types of praxis:

Sequencing Praxis is the ability to know how to get things done in order. Some children have dressing problems because they can't sequence whether to put the undershirt or the shirt on first. Most motor tasks have some sequencing to them, so sequencing praxis is considered to be central to all praxis. It helps start us on our way to being organized.

Accommodations at School

·   Organize materials and put all supplies needed for a special activity into the same box or bag in his desk.

·   Label the box or bag according to the activity.

·   At the end of each activity have him replace the supplies in the bag before going on to the next activity.

·   In extreme cases, number or letter the items in their order of use so he will know and can find the next tool to be used.

Accommodations at Home

·   Lay out the child's pieces of clothing in the order in which they are to be put on.

·   Make a list of regular activities and place them beside the bed or in the bathroom for easy reference.

·   Organize tools and materials in the order in which they are to be used (as pieces of flatware are placed on the table in the order in which they are to be used—you use the farthest fork first).

· Make a list of the order in which one should prepare for school.

Praxis on verbal command is the ability to give a motor response to a verbal command. For example, if a child is given a direction to "sit down and pick up your pencil," he has to hear two steps and complete two motor acts.

Accommodations

· Give one-step directions
· Wait until the first step is completed before giving another direction

Postural Praxis is the ability to imitate body position. Individuals with this difficulty are often poor at sports or games. If the instructor says, "Hold the bat like this," the individual may have greater difficulty than average in grasping how to place the body or to move.

Accommodations

· If occupational therapy is available, refer the child for assessment.
· Have the physical education teacher prepare a group of gross motor activities that can be practiced at recess and while the child is on the playground.
· Talk with the parents/teacher about a close friend or "buddy" to assist him with his workout.
· Send the list home for a workout there.

Oral Praxis is the ability to organize sequenced movements in the area of the mouth. It is often a problem area for children with speech difficulties. They may be unable to coordinate the teeth, tongue and vocal chords to sound out the syllables once they have deciphered the word. This form of praxis is usually addressed by the speech and language therapist at your child's school.

Constructional Praxis requires the manipulation of objects in three dimensions of space. Difficulty in this area may be seen as difficulty folding paper so that both sides are even and inability to stack blocks or books above a certain level without knocking the whole thing down.

Accommodations

·   Teach the child to play jacks; assign a buddy to help him with practice.

·   Play a game in which the child has to stack objects. Make the game one in which he has to best his last effort

·   Give points that can be redeemed for a prize for each five points of improvement each week.

Balance

Just as the eyes are the sensory organs for sight and the nose is the sensory organ for smell, the inner ear is the sensory organ for balance. The inner ear has a great influence on balance and eye movements as well as influence over muscle tone. (See Chapter II The Vestibular System).

Indirectly, inner ear problems are thought to have a marked influence on learning, in part because of the vestibular system's profound control over the neck and eyes. This system is the reason inner ear infections in children receive so much attention from pediatricians and complaints of earaches should receive immediate medical attention.   Children experiencing a problem with balance will often be clumsy, appear to trip over their own feet and may experience frequent falls. While sitting, they may squirm in their seat or even fall off their chair onto the floor. Although not as easily identified, children who run or are constantly on the move may also have a balance problem. Running actually requires less balance than walking slowly. In extreme cases, being unable to balance to stop, children occasionally race along and then slide onto the ground as if sliding into home plate.

Accommodations/Modifications

·   Have the child's ears checked for an inner ear infection, water from swimming or an accident that may have affected the inner ear.

Postural Insecurity results in a fear of falling because of an inability to keep one's balance. With growth and time, these individuals may have acquired balance that is adequate for normal activity, but because of the time when they were unbalanced, they remain so fearful of falling that they won't attempt new activities.

Gross Motor Control

Gross motor control refers to the ability to make large, general movements (such as waving an arm or lifting a leg). It requires the proper integration of muscle and nerve function. Gross motor control is a milestone in the development of an infant. As an infant's neurological system matures, he or she is able to refine unintentional, random, uncontrolled movements. Maturation is assisted by active physical activity, which requires large muscle movement. If the child is clumsy and bumps into things or is uncoordinated and poor at sports, begin by increasing physical activity. [xxxii]

Accommodations

· Play games that require running, track and field-type relays and sprinting. This is great for encouraging the development of gross motor coordination.

· Wanting to climb is an innate characteristic of children; this is why every playground has a sliding board and other objects to climb on. If you don't have similar play structures at home, take your child to the park or playground and let him climb on the jungle gym or other structures designed for gross motor development. At each visit he will get a little better because he is developing those important gross motor muscles.

· Hopping: Have a competition to see how long he can hop on one foot. All that hopping is developing some balance.

· Play Ball: Kick, catch, throw. Kicking, rolling and throwing are great ways to encourage gross motor development and you don't need anything more than a ball and a little bit of room. Nerf balls are excellent for indoor exercise. Turn a safe space in your home into a gym for one hour each evening.

· Batting: Get out the baseball bat and polish up your batting skills. This is a hard one for kids to master, but well worth the reward. Try a bigger, thicker bat to start with and work your way up to a smaller one.

If there is no improvement with lots of outdoor physical activity such as running, jumping, skipping and hopping, which develop balance and coordination, there is a more serious problem and it is time for a professional evaluation.

Designing the Individualized Education Plan

Children with sensori-motor immaturity may become frustrated easily and may seem manipulative and controlling. Some may try to compensate with an over-reliance on language and may prefer fantasy games to real life. They also may try to mask their motor planning problems by acting like a "class clown" or avoiding new group activities.

They may have difficulty with reading or handwriting; may have poor gross motor skills or may have become a behavioral problem.

These children might appear to be bored, unmotivated, troublesome or stubborn. Regardless, the end result is often low self-esteem, which negatively influences achievement. Many children with these problems seem unhappy. When a child sees, feels or hears things differently and is being disciplined for this, it tends to be hard on his ego. It is natural for others to expect him to react as others do, but he can't; his behavior is often not under his control. A bright child may know something is not right and not understand why. He may begin compensating for his differences by avoiding tasks that are hard or embarrassing.

Modifications and accommodations have been offered above for the multiple ways in which problems with sensori-motor integration are evidenced in the classroom. Here are some additional things that you as the parent should insist upon. It is the school's job to figure out who, when and how to get it done. Remember, these things are appropriate for your child and the law entitles you to them.

- Ask that physical education activities be therapeutic in nature.
- Teach the child to put his hand on the seat of the chair before sitting down.
- If your school district has occupational therapy, inquire to see if your child is eligible for the service.
- Insist that your child not be kept in at recess and that he be encouraged to engage in gross motor activities during that time.
- Insist that your child not be required to read aloud in class if doing so is embarrassing.
- Ensure that your child is not laughed at, scolded or ridiculed for being different.

·   Insist that all factors be considered prior to discipline; a student's behavior is a cry for help.

·   Instead of discipline, the child should be counseled to understand his sensory immaturity and explore ways in which to compensate.

The classroom teacher should be able to outline exactly what your child needs to do to achieve in his classroom. You should demand that the school identify specific strengths and weaknesses of your child. If they are at a loss, ask for an evaluation by the school psychologist. Be sure to emphasize that you are looking for strengths and weaknesses in learning, not eligibility for special education.

In this area more than any other, you need to know the specific strengths and weaknesses of your child so that an appropriate IEP can be designed.

CHAPTER XVII

ATTENTION

Attention is described as the ability to focus selectively on a stimulus, sustaining that focus and shifting it at will, or the ability to concentrate. A common misconception about children with attention problems is that they aren't paying attention at all. Actually, children who struggle with attention may pay attention to everything; their difficulty is deciding what to focus on and maintaining that focus.

For a child in a classroom, paying attention to the teacher requires filtering out as many as 30 other students, chairs scraping against the floor, the pencil sharpener, the phone ringing and multiple conversations. Add to that the visual stimuli of chalkboards, pictures, posters, bulletin boards, the faces of 30 students inside the classroom, the weather, children playing, the principal approaching, a dog outside the classroom window and students passing in the hallway. Out of all these sources of stimulation, the child is expected to hear the teacher and not only focus upon, but concentrate on her/his voice and hear the details in a series of multi-step instructions.

Many children have difficulty managing this challenge. Those who have the greatest difficulty are considered to have an attention deficit. Attention deficits cover a range from mild to severe and may be accompanied by hyperactivity.

Let's begin by exploring the difference between attention the learning disability and attention deficit disorder which are not classified as learning disabilities. The difference is primarily due to the source of professionals who defined the disorder. Attention Deficit Disorder and Attention Deficit Disorder with Hyperactivity were defined by the American Psychological Association and focus on behaviors, thereby making them behavioral disorders. Attention as the learning disability was defined by the Department of Education and focuses on learning.

As outlined in the chapter on visual processing, children with immature visual development will begin to exhibit signs of inattention as they reach levels of extreme fatigue. Proper diagnosis depends upon what the child may be experiencing at the time the behavior is exhibited. Proper identification of the contributing factors helps direct parents and teachers to more appropriate interventions.

Because attention is a complex process within the central nervous system there are several areas where signs of struggle may appear. If any of these signs occur inconsistently or in a particular subject area, they may be pointing to a problem other than attention. When children struggle with reading, for example, it is very difficult for them to concentrate and stay focused when they have not mastered the basics or they have difficulties with vision.

The control of one's attention has been identified as consisting of three systems: mental energy, processing and production. Some experience problems with all of these attention systems, while others may show strengths and weaknesses in different systems.

The Mental Energy System[liii]

The mental energy system regulates and distributes the energy supply needed for the brain to take in and interpret information and regulate behavior. Children whose mental energy is not working effectively may become mentally fatigued when they try to concentrate or they may exhibit other problems related to maintaining the brain energy needed for optimal learning and behavior. There are four mental energy controls:

Alertness, is a state of mind in which a child can effectively listen to and watch information being presented. Children who experience difficulty with alertness can appear to be daydreaming.

Sleep and arousal balance is a state of mind that affects the ability to sleep well enough at night to be sufficiently alert during the day. Children who are experiencing trouble with sleep and arousal may find it difficult to get to sleep at night or they may sleep poorly. They then have trouble getting up in the morning and may appear tired in class. (Additional information on this subject is presented in the chapter on Sleep and Learning).

Mental effort initiates and maintains the flow of energy required for a child to start, work on and complete a task. Mental effort is particularly important when children are faced with tasks that they do not personally find motivating. Children who have difficulty with mental effort can benefit from having tasks broken down into smaller, more manageable parts.

Performance consistency works to ensure a reliable, predictable flow of energy from moment to moment and day to day. Children who have trouble with performance consistency don't have problems all the time; sometimes they can concentrate and perform well, while at other times they cannot. Their work output and behavior may be impossible to predict.

Signs and Symptoms of Mental Energy deficit:
- Has difficulty concentrating; may complain of feeling tired or bored.
- Does not seem to be well-rested and fully awake during the day
- Inconsistent work patterns that negatively impact quality and quantity of work
- Shows over-activity and fidgets; especially pronounced when sitting and listening

Accommodations/Modifications at School
- Make eye or physical contact to sustain attention.
- Provide frequent short breaks.
- Encourage physical activity; arrange for him to move about the room.

- Give the child permission to move about when he is tired.
- Seat the child next to the teacher.

Accommodations/Modifications at Home

- Have a consistent bedtime schedule; see that the child gets enough sleep.
- Help the child to recognize when he is most focused.
- Talk with the teacher about scheduling important activities during these times.
- Shorten the child's school day.
- Let him finish assignments at home.

The Processing System

The processing system helps a child select, prepare and begin to interpret incoming information. Children who have difficulty with processing may have a range of problems related to regulating the use of incoming information. There are five processing controls.

Saliency determination involves selecting which incoming information is the most important. Children who have difficulty with this control may be distracted by things that aren't relevant and may miss important information being presented.

Depth and detail of processing controls how intensely children can concentrate on highly specific data. It enables them to focus deeply enough to recognize and remember necessary details.

Cognitive activation connects new information to what has already been learned through prior knowledge and experience. Children who are inactive processors are unable to connect to prior knowledge to assist their understanding of new information. In contrast, overactive processors are reminded of too much prior knowledge, making it difficult for them to maintain focus.

Focal maintenance allows a child to focus on important information for an appropriate period of time. Some children who don't concentrate long enough on certain things may concentrate too long on others. The important factor is not how long the attention span is, but how well matched it is with the demands of the task at hand.

Satisfaction control involves a child's ability to allocate enough attention to activities or topics of moderate or low levels of interest.

Signs and symptoms of difficulty with processing:

· Processes too little or too much information; can't distinguish between what is and what is not important.

· Focuses too superficially or too deeply on information presented

Accommodations/Modifications at School

· Write important points or directions on the board.

· Have child highlight and/or color code important ideas.

· Summarize main ideas before beginning next topic.

· Simplify content of lessons.

· Break tasks into smaller steps; complete the first step before giving the second.

· Connect new information with previously learned information.

· Stand in front of and make eye contact with the child when giving instructions.

· Keep a schedule of activities on the board for child to refer to.

· Cue child to upcoming transitions.

Accommodations/Modifications at Home

· Allow extra processing time; get started early for trips and family outings.

· Monitor the child to estimate a rate of maximal output.

· Allow extra time for completion of homework.

Production

Production governs output, including what children generate academically, behaviorally and socially. Children with production control problems have a range of difficulties related to regulating academic and behavioral output. They may do things too quickly without thinking, planning or previewing outcomes. There are five production controls:

Previewing involves considering more than one action or response and anticipating the likely outcome of a particular choice. Observed behavior: may plunge into activities instantly and react too quickly.

Facilitation and inhibition is the ability to exercise restraint and not act immediately, to consider multiple options and to choose the best one before acting or starting on a task. Observed behavior: frequently acts impulsively and may appear to be doing only the first thing that comes to mind or may blurt out answers before being called upon in class.

Pacing means doing tasks or activities at the most appropriate speed. Pacing difficulties often show up in children's reading. Their reading pace may be so fast that they skip over words, have difficulty with multi-syllable words and show little reading comprehension.

Self-monitoring allows children to evaluate how they are doing while performing and after completing a task. This control allows children to regulate their attention and take corrective action.

The ability to use prior learning enables children to use previous experience to guide current behavior and approaches to current tasks. Often called hindsight, this ability enables children to make use of precedent, experience and prior knowledge to guide their decision-making and actions.

Signs and Symptoms of Difficulty with Production

· Has difficulty coming up with the right strategy or technique to accomplish a task

· Does not monitor quality of work or the effectiveness of strategies

· Does not use past successes and failure to guide current behavior, actions, or strategies

· Is apt to do too many things too quickly and some other things too slowly

· Has a poor sense of time and how to manage it

Accommodations at School

· Help the child plan his project before beginning.

· Use a "To Do" list to keep track of assignments.

· Reduce the amount of work to be completed.

· Give credit for the work completed; do not deduct for unfinished work.

· Teach children to self-monitor—"amount I can get done in five minutes."

Accommodations at Home

·   Assist the child in preparing an assignment.

·   Teach him the steps in the process.

·   Negotiate a longer time to complete reports.

·   Teach child to grade his own work, and then correct it before turning it in.

This extensive description of all the factors influencing a child's ability to attend in the classroom dictates the need for a rather definitive diagnosis of the specific nature of the child's strengths and weaknesses in each of these areas. The specific nature of the disability has to be identified in order to design classroom accommodations and interventions that will make his education "appropriate."

What to Do

Have regular conversations with your child's teacher. Information from both home and school environments is perquisite to an accurate diagnosis of the child's learning problem. Working together, parents, teachers and the child himself can inform one another about how best to address the child's needs.

Careful observation at home should document whether the child is as inattentive in front of the TV as he is in the classroom. Children with true neuro-cognitive deficits are inattentive all the time. If the inattention and or hyperactivity are situational, then there is a different learning problem.

Take care to note whether he is as hyperactive at 9 a.m. as he is at 2 p.m. If his behavior varies from normal in the morning to hyper in the afternoon, he does not have an attention deficit; rather, he may be experiencing a breakdown in attention due to fatigue, resulting from some other problem such as a visual processing deficit or poor nutrition.

Your friendly school psychologist is the one who should identify the exact nature of the problem. However, in most instances school psychologists are not trained to do this kind of diagnosis and special education is not presently designed to provide this sort of appropriateness to children's education and teacher education programs are not presently preparing teachers to request this sort of information when designing classroom instruction.

Therefore, with this document in hand you, the parent, are going to make a difference in the way your child experiences these circumstances by making the school aware of this information and requesting their cooperation in observing for significant behaviors. This information will lead to identifying possible environmental factors contributing to your child's changing ability to stay focused. When the school becomes aware of what you are trying to accomplish, they will come on board and fulfill their part in identifying the contributing factors. All the information needed to accomplish this objective is included in this manual (See Advocacy, and Advocacy at its Best).

Let the professionals in the field take on the entire educational system; you are concerned with just one child—yours. Your child needs you at home to modify his diet, see that he gets enough sleep and to do the experimentation needed to find the specific cause of the problem.

CHAPTER XVIII

ATTENTION DEFICIT DISORDER

Attention Deficit Disorder, while not identified or defined as a learning disability, is included here because of the misperceptions between it and attention the learning disability. Further, it is one of the most misunderstood and misdiagnosed of the disabling conditions affecting children.

If attention deficit disorder is a label currently attached to your child or a child you care about, discussion here will help with formulating questions, understanding the nature of the disability, current forms of treatment and interventions to accommodate the disorder at home and in the classroom.

ADD, ADHD Defined

According to the Diagnostic and Statistical Manual of Mental Disorders, Fourth Edition (DSM-IV)—a standard reference source published by the American Psychological Association—there are three patterns of behavior that indicate ADHD: inattention, hyperactivity and difficulty controlling one's actions. Signs of inattention as outlined in DSM-IV include:

· becoming easily distracted by irrelevant sights and sounds
· failing to pay attention to details and making careless mistakes
· rarely following instructions carefully
· losing or forgetting things like toys, pencils, books and tools needed for a task

Signs of hyperactivity and impulsivity are described as

· feeling restless, often fidgeting with hands or feet, squirming
· running, climbing or leaving a seat in a situation when sitting or quiet behavior is expected
· blurting out an answer before hearing the whole question
· having difficulty waiting in line or taking a turn

Because everyone shows some of these behaviors at times, the DSM-IV contains very specific guidelines for determining when they indicate ADHD. The behaviors must appear early in life, before age 7, and continue for at least six months. In children, they must be more frequent or severe than in others the same age. Above all, the behaviors must create a real handicap in at least two areas of the person's life, such as at school, home, work or in social settings. A child with some attention problems, but whose school work or friendships are not impaired by these behaviors, would not be diagnosed with ADHD, nor would a child who seems overly active at school but functions well elsewhere.

If the lack of attention impacts only school and does not negatively impact home, work or social settings, the child would be diagnosed by the school psychologist as being eligible for special education because of a processing disorder in attention. The difference is in frequency, duration and the extent to which the disability exhibits itself across settings.

The psychological and medical communities as a whole have accepted the DSM-IV criteria for diagnosing chronic attention problems. However, this term and its use in diagnosis remains controversial and the approaches to attention problems are varied. The diversity of views comes in part from the fact that although paying attention may seem like an isolated task, it is an elaborate integration of many systems within the central nervous system.

Additionally, the term looks only at behavior, without consideration of the factors contributing to the behavior. A child with a perfectly healthy nervous system will begin to exhibit hyperactive behavior when he experiences one of a number of environmental stressors. When the stressor is removed the behavior returns to normal.

Keep in mind that ADHD is not a label that describes a child's ability to learn and therefore is not considered a condition or label recognized by the Department of Education as being eligible for special education. It may be helpful to keep in mind, also, that specific behaviors exhibited by a child are not as important as why the child is exhibiting the behavior.

Lack of Sleep

Sleep deprivation can cause daytime hyperactivity and decrease in focused attention. This can be mistaken for Attention Deficit Hyperactivity Disorder (ADHD) or other behavior disorders. Therefore, it should not be concluded that children who have ADHD have difficulty sleeping. Rather, the truth of the matter is that children who experience a lack of sleep exhibit an inability to stay focused and may become hyperactive.

Some experts say as many as 70-80% of all patients with ADHD have difficulty sleeping; by far, the most common complaint is not being able to fall asleep. One study showed that patients with ADHD vary nightly on how long it takes to fall asleep by as much as two to three hours, while those without ADHD normally fell asleep within 40 minutes.

Problems sleeping can cause symptoms such as fatigue, having difficulty concentrating, being easily distracted, and experiencing hyperactivity, headaches and anxiety. Many symptoms of sleep disorders can mimic symptoms of ADHD. It is important, therefore, to discuss sleep patterns with your doctor and determine if treatment is necessary for the sleep disorder as well as the ADHD. Medical treatment, although important, should go hand-in-hand with developing good sleeping habits.

Diet vs. Medication

The feud between professions regarding the effects of diet on behavior has been raging for over fifty years. However, observant parents have long realized that the consumption of food additives causes hyperactivity in their child, while most conventional doctors do not support this line of thought.

When you feed your child processed foods containing additives and artificial colors, you are introducing toxic chemicals into his bloodstream. Those chemicals find their way into the brain and alter brain function. In the case of a child who has been diagnosed with ADHD, the chemicals have alter his behavior and made him restless with a shortened attention span. But the culprit isn't just food additives; it is also refined carbohydrates.

Hyperactivity and restlessness are caused primarily by lack of sleep and diet. Consider soft drinks, refined white flour, loads of refined white sugar and plenty of fried foods and processed foods to boot (a Big Mac, French fries, and a Coke). Take a child off these manufactured substances, resolve his sleep-related problems and start feeding him real food and the "disease" of ADHD vanishes in a matter of weeks. This has been succinctly demonstrated through clinical studies, which found that dietary changes completely eliminated the so-called disease of ADHD in some children.[liv] For other children, addressing the sleep-related problems and allergies also eliminated the symptoms.

As it turns out, the refined sugars may cause behavioral disorders by depleting the body of the B vitamins and several notable minerals, including magnesium and zinc, which are required for neurological health. When the human body is deficient in these vitamins and minerals, it will exhibit both mental and physical disorders. (See Nutrition, Allergies and Hypoglycemia).

The other approach to the problem is to medicate rather than diagnose and eliminate contributing causes. There is much evidence that the medications used to treat ADHD have a significant negative impact upon behavior and impede growth.

Ponder this news story, entitled "Boom in Ritalin Sales Raises

Ethical Issues." The story begins, "The stimulant Ritalin treats the needs of health professionals, parents and teachers rather than the needs of children." Attention Deficit Disorder is identified as a "disease," while its identification and/or diagnosis is dependent upon a list of symptoms that include such behaviors as "often fidgets with hands or feet or squirms in seat," 'often leaves seat in classroom or in other situations in which remaining seated is expected" and "often has difficulty awaiting a turn."

Many factors could lead a child to behave in this manner, including a spirited, creative nature that defies conformity, inconsistent discipline or lack of unconditional love, boring and oversized classrooms, an overstressed teacher, lack of teacher attention to individual educational needs, anxiety due to abuse or neglect at home or elsewhere, conflict and communication problems in the family and misguided educational and behavioral expectations for the child. (These concerns are covered at length in Part I of this manual, Chapter II through VIII).

Many such children are energetic, creative and independent youngsters struggling within the constraints of a negligent, inattentive, conflicted or stressed adult environment. It seems, therefore, that Attention Deficit Disorder, at least in some cases, might not reflect a child's attention deficits as much as they might reflect our lack of attention to his needs.

If Attention Deficit Disorder is identified by a list of behaviors, does it follow logically that we burn out his brain with drugs rather than take him off the sugar, refined white flour and food additives, which are known causes of the behaviors, as well as other well-known environmental factors such as a lack of sleep?

Ritalin does not correct biochemical imbalances, it causes them; there is some evidence that it can cause permanent damage to the child's brain and its function. Pediatricians, parents and teachers are not aware of these hazards because a large body of research demonstrating the ill-effects of this drug has been ignored and suppressed in order to encourage the sale of the drug. Damaging effects of the drug can include:[xxxiii]

·   Decreased blood flow to the brain, causing impaired thinking ability and memory loss
·   Disruption of growth hormone, leading to suppression of growth in

the body and brain

·   Permanent neurological tics, including Tourette's syndrome (this author could not embrace this concept until experiencing working with a child with Ritalin-induced neurological tics. His parent confirmed the origin of the problem with a doctor's report.)

·   Addiction and abuse, including withdrawal reactions

·   Psychosis (mania), depression, insomnia, agitation and social withdrawal, possible shrinkage (atrophy) or other permanent physical abnormalities in the brain—the very symptoms the drug is supposed to improve

·   Decreased ability to learn

·   Increased hyperactivity and inattention

·   Death due to interference with heart function

Ritalin and other stimulants are currently prescribed to several million U.S. children in the hope of improving their alleged hyperactivity, inattention and impulsivity. There is evidence that these drugs "work" by producing robotic or zombie-like behavior in children. This enforced docility can produce a few weeks of subdued behavior and obedience, but has no positive effect on academic achievement and no positive long-term effects at all. Contrary to claims by drug advocates, giving Ritalin to a child does not help to prevent future problems such as school failure or delinquency.

Ritalin's lack of effectiveness has been proven by hundreds of studies but has not been revealed to doctors, teachers or parents. Parents, teachers and even doctors have been badly misled by drug company marketing practices, and children are suffering as a result.

There are thousands of resources providing information necessary to empower parents to help their children with their behavioral and school problems without resorting to drugs. Mind-altering drugs are never an appropriate approach to helping children. Instead, it is encouraged that parents become involved and learn to identify and meet the individual needs of the children in their care.

Most children receiving Ritalin have been identified for treatment by teachers who have been misled by drug companies and government promotional campaigns for Ritalin and other stimulants. The stimulant drugs include Ritalin (methylphenidate), Dexedrine and Dextrostat (dextroamphetamine or d-amphetamine), Adderall (D-amphetamine and amphetamine mixtures), Desoxyn and Gradumet (methamphetamine) and Cylert (pemoline).

A Horror Story

Believe it or not, until recently it has been perfectly legal for schools to force school children to be put on psychoactive mind-altering drugs as a condition of attending that school. That is, the counselor or school administrator could insist that a certain child be dosed with mind-altering drugs. It sounds bizarre but was absolutely true until just recently.

Congress finally has passed legislation that bans schools from forcing parents to drug their children for behavioral problems. On December 3, 2004, the Individuals with Disabilities Education Improvement Act (IDEA) was signed into law by President Bush. Incorporated within this act was the first of its kind Federal legislation called the "Prohibition on Mandatory Medication Amendment." This new law prohibits schools from recommending or requiring that a child take a controlled substance in order to attend school. (The law includes all stimulants—Ritalin, Adderall, Concerta, Dexedrine, Dextrostat, etc.)

Now you may think, "Gee, this isn't a problem; I never heard about this." But in fact, it was a huge problem. There have been many cases in which children were denied an education because their parents refused to put them on narcotic stimulants, antidepressants or other drugs that we now know cause violent behavior and increased risk of suicide. And in extreme cases these drugs actually caused or contributed to the kind of mass murder that we saw in Columbine, when two high school students picked up assault rifles, went to school and assaulted teachers and classmates. These two kids were on antidepressant drugs—it's still one of the most censored stories of the last decade.[xxxiv]

Ritalin earns millions of dollars per year for drug companies, which have a very strong lobby in Washington, D.C. It is a wonder that Congress finally banned schools' rights to demand that a child be drugged in order to receive a public education. It seems more reasonable that they would have banned the drug that is poisoning children and stunting their growth.

What to Do

You will have to be the judge of the age-old feud between nutrition and medication for ADHD; maybe you can do some research yourself.

As a parent you have to get serious about preparing the body and brain of your child to be ready for learning. A child who regularly consumes soft drinks and junk food and does not sleep well is a child who is not biologically prepared to learn.

On the individual level, your child needs your time and energy. Nothing can replace the personal relationship your child needs with you, his parent or primary caretaker. An active interest in the welfare of your child, observation of his behavior and some experimentation in the kitchen will provide your own evidence regarding the impact of nutrition on your child's behavior.

If your child is hyperactive, read the chapter on nutrition and change your dietary habits. Cook real food. Don't drug your child into stunted growth and brain damage. Get involved with your child. If the school is giving your child Ritalin, you should know it without being told. If they insist that your child be drugged, get mad, and say, no! Then go home and cook him a nutritious meal, take the TV out of his room and see that he gets to sleep early.

If after three or four weeks the hyperactivity is no longer in evidence, you can congratulate yourself for being a good parent and take a long, restful vacation with all the money you will have saved by not having to buy any more Ritalin. Real fruits and vegetables are far less expensive. Just think—no more time out of your busy schedule to attend IEPs.

If he is already on the drug, insist that he be withdrawn gradually as you find the time to prepare nutritious meals. Be prepared for a difficult time; drug withdrawal can be painful and challenging and should be supervised by a physician.

Impact of Allergies on Drawings of six Year Old
Boy
Vestibular Apparatus

---

[i] The masculine gender is used throughout this text because boys more often than girls present with learning disabilities. However, the information presented here is equally applicable to both males and females.

[ii] Dunnigan, Timothy Ph.D., Clinical Psychologist, www.helpforfamilies.com

[iii] Levin, Cynthia, Psy., Professional Interview with Daniel Siegel, M.D., Http://MentalHelp.net

[iv] T. Berry Brazelton, M. D., Pediatrician, Specialist Child Development.

[5] Perry, G.D, Neurobiological Sequelae of Childhood Trauma: Post Traumatic Stress Disorders in Children. IN: Catecholamine Function in Post Traumatic Stress Disorder: Emerging Concepts. Pp. 32-37, (M. Murburg. Ed.)

[6] www.childtrauma.org/ctaamaterials/ptsdchild. American Psychiatric Press, Washington, DC., pp. 253-276, 1994

[7] www.helpguide.org/mental/emotinal_psychological_trauma.html Emotional and psychological Trauma: Causes, Symptoms, Effects and Treatment

[8] Santa Barbara Graduate Institute, Symptoms of Emotional Trauma. www.traumaresources.org/emotional_trauma_overview.html

[9] www.traumaresources.ort/emotional_trauma.

[10] Traumaresources.org

[11] www.apa.org/practice/traumaticstress.html. The American Psychological Association

[12] A Report and Policy Agenda. Helping Traumatized Children Learn   Massachusetts Advocates for Children, 1005, www.massadvocates.org/helping_traumatized_children_learn

[13] Pollitt & Gorman, 1994, Nutritional deficiencies as developmental risk factors. In Nelson, C.A. (Ed) Threats to optimal development integrating biological, psychological and social risk factors. Hilldale NJ: Lawrence Erlbaum Associates Publishers

[14] This section is summarized in its entirety from: Weintraub, 1997: Natural treatments for ADD and hyperactivity. Pleasant Grove, UT: Woodland Publishing, pp. 101-104. www.ilt.co.za

[15] www.healthday.com/view.cfm?id-518225

[16] Rapp, D.J. 1996, Is this your child's world? How you can fix the schools and homes that are making your children sick. New York: Bantam Book

[17] Integrated Learning Therapy at www.ilt.co.za

[18] Penland, James G. Ph.D., US Department of Agriculture. www.gfhnrc.ars.usda.gov/

[19] Nutrition.about.com

[20] Kid shealth.org/kid/stay_healthy/food/breakfast.html

[21] Pivik, T.T., Dykman, R.A., Badger, T.M. 2005. Eating or Skipping Breakfast: Effects on Resting EEG Activity and Heart Rate. Federation of American Societies for Experimental Biology Conference V.19 (4). Paper No. 275.3, March 2005

[21] www.sleepfoundation.org/SleepinAmericaPoll

[22] www.drgreene.com

[23] sleepfoundation.org/SleepinAmericaPoll

[24] sleepfoundation.org/SleepinAmericaPoll

[25] Blunden, S. et.al, 2000. Journal of Clinical & Experimental Neuropsychology, Vol 22(5) 664-668

[26] Journal of Pediatric Psychology, June 1997

[27] www.kidshealth.org/parent/growth/sleep/bedtime_basics.html

[28] www.mercurypoisoned.com

29 International Academy of Oral Medicine & Toxicology)   www.iamomt.org//index.cfm April 6 2005

30 www.iaomt.org//index.cfm. California Bans Thimerosal from Vaccines.

31 www.rlaurathompson.com/heavy_metal_toxicity.html

32 Balch, James F., and Balch, Phyllis A., Prescription for Nutritional Healing, Avery Publishing Group Inc., Garden City park, New York 1999

33 www.angelhealingcenter.com/CilantroPestoRecipe

34 www.ed.gov/parents/needs/speced/iepguide/index A Guide to the Individualized Education program, U.S. Department of Education, with the assistance of the National Information Center for Children and Youth with Disabilities

35 www.nfpanc.org. Foster Parent Educational Advocacy Training

36 Naglieri, J. A. (2003). "Current Advances in Assessment and Intervention for Children with Learning Disabilities." In T. E. Scruggs and M.A. Mastropieri (Eds.) Advances in Learning and Behavioral Disabilities Volume 16: Identification and Assessment (pp. 163-190) New York: JAI.

37 Excerpts from an article by Larry Falxa, which appeared in the Spring '93 Newsletter of the Greater Rochester Attention Deficit Disorder Association. http://gradda.home.isp-direct.com/sp93wood.html

38 McManis, Mary www.visionandlearning.org

39 www.childrenandvision.com

40 National Center for Learning Disabilities www.ldonline.org

41 Summarized from Novak, Laura, Not Austic or Hyperactive, Just Seeing Double at Times. New York times, September 11, 2007

42 www.ldonline.org/ld(indepth/process_deficit/visual_audiory.html)

43 Sensory Systems Clinic, P.C. www.sensorysystemsclinic.com

44 www.nidcd.nih.gov National Institute on Deafness and Other Communication Disorders

45 Ibid

46 Misunderstood Minds, Public Broadcasting System, WGBH www.pbs.org/wgbh/misunderstoodminds.

47 www.retrainthebrain.com/index.html

48 Misunderstood Minds, Public Broadcasting System, WGBH www.pbs.org/wgbh/misunderstoodminds

49 www.paperpenalia.com/handwriting

50 Lamb, Gary www.musicintheclassroom.com

51 Your Child's Brain, Newsweek, February 19, 1996

52 Gunthe, Emily Diane, Super Learning 2000

53 www.allkindsofminds.org. by Dr. Mel Levine

54 NewsTarget.com (Ritalin, posted Marc 7, 2005

55 Breggin, Peter R., M.D., Talking Back to Ritalin, Common Courage Press, 1998

56 Breggin, Peter R., M.D., Talking Back to Ritalin, Common Courage Press, 1998